The Key to Keys

5 Steps to Developing an Effective Access Control Program

Randy Neely

BOOK CATEGORY: NON-FICTION

The Key to Keys
5 Steps to Developing an Effective Access Control Program

By Randy Neely

Copyright © 2016 RANDY NEELY, ALL RIGHTS RESERVED
info@KeytoKeys.com
www.KeytoKeys.com

ALL RIGHTS RESERVED. No part of this publication may be reproduced, distributed, or transmitted in any form or by any means, including photocopying, recording, or other electronic or mechanical methods, without prior written permission of the author, except in the case of brief quotations embodied in critical reviews and certain other noncommercial uses permitted by copyright law. For permission requests, write the author at the email address above.

ISBN: 978-1537234755

First Edition 2016

PUBLISHED BY:
10-10-10 Publishing
MARKHAM, ON
CANADA

Contents

Dedication	v
Acknowledgements	vii
Foreword	xi
PART I	1
I: Why This Book? Who Cares?	3
II: Core Goals of a Key Control Program	7
III: Evolution of Key Control Programs	25
IV: True Stories	31
V: Other Headlines Worth Pondering	39
VI: Macro View of Users	47
VII: Components of a Successful Key Control Program	55
PART II	61
VIII: Inventing the Solution	63
Epilogue	97
About the Author	102

I dedicate this book to:

Anne – my amazing, patient, encouraging wife and a tough *but* reasonable client – Te amo. Thank you!

Jim Diaz – A security operations colleague of mine that shared my frustration about lost keys and was my sounding board for many of the early years. Jim and I would talk about the technology that didn't exist, as solutions to the issue – Rest in Peace, JD.

Acknowledgements

I would like to express my gratitude to the many people that were a part of my experience contained in this book; to those that supported and encouraged me to keep pushing forward and "take the risk".

Thank you **Dennis Hammonds** for all of your time, hard work and encouragement in getting this idea off the ground! Your lessons in logistics were extremely eye-opening to me, by the way.

Our first *"Friends and Family"* fundraising Round - Thank you - **Dennis & Carol; Rocky & Christy; Brian & Cindy** and **Todd & Tara** – without all of you, my napkin drawing would still be sitting in my desk drawer collecting dust!

John Suryan – Dedicated CEO & Angel Investor - Thank you for "***getting it***", believing in it, investing in it and becoming the CEO of it! I now know why coaches and start-up entrepreneurs suggested I find someone to run the company that understands investing and starting up companies. Not only did you meet that criteria, but you understood the pain of the commercial property industry too – A home run for Tether Technologies. We've been through a lot in this endeavor and I cannot thank you enough for your patience and stick-to-it-ness this whole time – I've needed the grounding.

Sam Traff – The Money Man - Don't know how you do it, but without your contacts, business savvy and perseverance, this wouldn't have been possible – Thank you!

Randy Neely

Keith Kirkwood, Principal – Kirkwood Product Development – For understanding the concept and shrinking it to what our customers wanted. The v2 design has been both aesthetically pleasing and mechanically dependable. Awesome job!

My sincerest thanks and appreciation to **all of our Angel Investors**. The good that you bring to those with an idea, but not the means to bring it to reality, changes the world. Without people like you, everything would be just plain vanilla.

The Keiritsu Forum – Your candid and thorough Due Diligence Report (and later update) gave others the confidence to invest in our business plan and helped immensely with our funding efforts. I thank both the Forum's angel members for seeing the need for a product like the *Gravity* and the Keiretsu Capital Fund for investing in our future. I now know how few start-ups meet the Forum's investment criteria and am honored to have been chosen as an investible company.

Marc Pirello – The Formula Man. You were the first step I took to make this idea a reality. Thank you for being there, for answering my Craigslist Ad and for understanding what my ultimate goal for the **ekt**® was and thank you for helping Rachel with her calculus homework!

Rachel Harbaugh for your loving support and editing help with this book.

Jerry Yamamoto and Drew Carlson - Slipstream Design – You guys took an indiscernible hand drawing of a "thing" and brought form and function to it. You were both very easy to work with, patient and you delivered!

Scott Theilman & Company of Product Creation Studio (PCS) in Seattle – taking the **ekt**® from a drawing to the real thing was literally seeing a dream come true. I knew we selected the right company of engineers – when we started working with you, you had a large space and a few engineers...over a short period of time we enjoyed watching PCS grow and now you're about out of room. Everyone wants your expertise. Congratulations!

Bert Schippers and Amer Hadzikadunic of Schippers & Crew, our contract manufacturer. Your flexibility in building out units in batches and carrying our company receivable has been nothing short of awesome. I cannot think of any other group of professionals that I would want working on my products. Thank you!

Big Bang Electrical, Bill Grant – You helped us get from "v2" to the *Gravity* key tether by assessing over 600 different naming possibilities. *The New Force of Certainty* thanks you for that.

Bryan Brewer of Funding Quest – For Business Plans 1 and 2, as well as a great Executive Summary. It's no wonder so many newbie entrepreneurs reach out to you for guidance and coaching – you know the ropes.

The Raymond Aaron Group and 10-10-10 Publishing for keeping me on track, especially **Cara**'s encouragement and kind words as I wrote draft after draft of this book.

Foreword

I feel privileged to have this opportunity to introduce you to Randy Neely's book *The Key to Keys*. His book is filled with important information, interesting true stories, funny experiences and valuable lessons.

The Key to Keys will reveal truths about the security industry and key control – **then & now**, that you may have not heard before. Through stories and experiences of clients, employees, and competitors, Randy shares his 40-year journey in the field and decades of searching for a way to keep his clients' properties more secure. He has been able to achieve huge success in his industry starting as a part-time Security Officer to President and CEO of a large regional security company. His career long lessons-learned now revealed to you through these pages.

Take inspiration from Randy's story and problem-solving invention - he shares his trek, experiences, and the skills he has gained with you so that you can apply them to your security program and future in key control.

Randy Neely

His dedication, passion for his work and great sense of humor are the secret to his success. Before you spend another dime on key control products, programs or protocols, you MUST READ this book.

Shirley Pierini, MBA, CPP, PCI
President International – American Society for Industrial Security - 2004

PART I

I. Why This Book? Who Cares?

The purpose of this book is to review and discuss various methodologies and protocols for issuing, tracking, retrieving and mitigating the loss of critical facility/building hard keys and access cards. It is about physical security and the steps that can and should be taken to prevent unauthorized access from lost or misplaced keys. More importantly, **it's about sharing what's been the missing link to key control ever since I began in this industry in 1977.**

If you are a janitor, security officer, building engineer, or property manager, then this book is for you. If you are in charge of the physical safety and security of others, then this book is **especially** for you.

The process for accounting for keys is age old - as is the risk of keys becoming lost or misplaced. Not too long ago the answer to lost keys was "cutting" new ones. Today, given heightened levels of security and awareness, most facility owners/managers move quickly to rekey. This is done to ensure the safety and security of the property's employees, tenants and guests. This book explores various procedures and technologies that keep our facility keys secure.

Having spent more than 35 years in the physical security space, I have many stories to share. It starts for me in late 1977, as a part-time security officer at a 43-acre resort hotel, and continues through 2015 as president & CEO of Northwest Protective Service. Even after NW Protective was acquired by Universal Protection Service, many of my headaches came from keys. The worry over when the next set of keys would be lost and what the consequences would be was akin to a migraine. But before I tell you about the best headache medicine ever invented, let's get one misconception about key control and "keys" out of the way...

"Hard keys are going away. Before you know it, everything is going to be electronic/card access or biometric, so we'll never have to rekey a facility or building. It won't matter if a key gets lost."

Don't hold your breath. Losing or misplacing keys, whether they're hard keys or card keys, is a breach of security. It doesn't necessarily mean that you're going to have to rekey a building. In fact, 99% of the time that keys are lost or misplaced, they're found. Sometimes they're found within minutes, other times, it takes hours (even days). In one of the True Stories I share later in this book, the Security Rover didn't realize he had lost his keys until he was called to open an office door for a tenant. The last time he remembered using his keys was at least two hours earlier. His key ring had both hard keys and a card key. In another one of the True Stories, **72 hours** elapsed before it was discovered that the keys had gone missing.

It is also worth stating that converting the world to electronic card access is not going to happen "before you know it". One of my colleagues told me the other day that he was issued his first "card key" in 1986, or more than 30 years ago. Rapid change in technologies (think LP to 8-track to cassette to CD to iPod to streaming) happen in the span of years, if not decades. What's holding access cards back? The cost of "traditional" locks and hard keys is fractional compared to electronic access platforms, equipment and software (many of which require an annual license fee). I don't see a "global conversion" in my lifetime or my kid's lifetime – so in the meantime – we need to protect all forms of access means (keys of all types).

The real issue here is that someone could be using a set of misplaced keys for hours and no one knows it. It's the security breach that is the problem, not the rekey. It is true, if your building has electronic card access and you've discovered that a card key is missing, you can shut that card off – you don't have to rekey the building. But the operative word here is "discovered".

It is also important to realize that whether your building has traditional hard key locks, electronic access cards or biometric access, the odds are that there is still a keyway in each door, in the event the electronics or biometric platform fail. Keys will be with us for a long time to come.

The last point I'll make regarding access cards is that employees tend to be a bit laxer. *"Why do I need to worry about losing my card when it can just be turned off?"* Perception, whether real or not, is that hard keys are more valuable than access cards. This is a perception that you absolutely want to fight, as misplacing any and all means of access is a bad thing.

While a lock breach to a building may not have resulted in loss, injury or death, Courts have found in many cases that protocols for managing key control programs must be "reasonable." Occupants or persons using the facility to secure their belongings, or selves, have a reasonable expectation of safety. Another "test" the Courts ask is "Was the breach foreseeable?" For example, if a key has been lost or unaccounted for in the past, a breach, while maybe not likely, could be foreseeable and therefore "preventable".

It's my intention that the following chapters will give you a map along with steps to follow to guide you in creating your key control plan, thereby avoiding costly pitfalls. Additionally, I think you'll find that the "punch line" to my book will give you the missing link to key control as we know it today and as we will know it for many years to come. For the foreseeable future, buildings will require the services of janitorial staff, maintenance or engineering workers, and in most cases, security officers. These people will be required to access multiple locations in a building – all with different risk factors.

Randy Neely

Whether the access they use is a hard-key or a card key – if they set the key(s) down and walk away or they misplace, lose or have them taken, we want to know as soon as possible. Every minute that the key(s) is unaccounted for, someone could be mis-using it and that shouldn't be. It is a huge risk that I've spent my entire career trying to mitigate.

II. Core Goals of a Key Control Program

There are simple lock & key installations and there are very large ones, requiring a significant amount of organization and documentation. Throughout this book, I will give examples that relate to *moderate-*sized programs; giving you exposure to many considerations.

While selecting and installing locks and keys may differ from a 500 sq. ft. building to a 1.2 MM sq. ft. building, the steps for maintaining and managing key controls are the same. Developing a key control program that scales from project to project is paramount.

We can all agree that there are different risk factors associated with different buildings or facilities. For example, building key controls for a structure that has four exterior doors and is used for storing low cost packing materials would be considered Low Risk. In comparison, a building that is used 24 hours per day, 7 days per week, as living quarters for people, would clearly be High Risk. A failure in maintaining strong key and access controls in this or any High Risk environment could result in personal injury or death of human lives.

There are other factors to consider as you build your key control program. How complex will your access map be? A simple access map might have a GM (Grand Master), Master (M), Sub-Master (Change Key) and of course, the door key. Each level of access (Grand Master, Master, Change Key) can be considered a "break". In this scenario, the lock system has 3 breaks (not including the individual door key). The more breaks you build into a lock system, the weaker the system becomes. I've been told 4 breaks is a good rule whenever possible. I have seen lock systems that have 6 breaks. The more breaks you have, the easier picking becomes by those that know how.

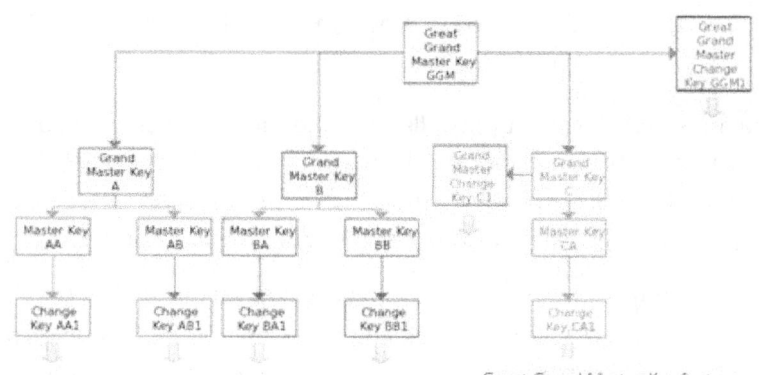

Great Grand Master Key System
By: Aaron Barlow

Identify Keys

When developing a key control program, documenting **what** keys you have and **how many** of each you'll need, is paramount. This means **ALL** keys – keys to:

Desks

File cabinets

Key box(es)

Lock box(es)

TV/AV equipment rack(s)

Clothes/personal lockers

Mailbox(es)

The Key to Keys

Storage rooms (i.e.: janitorial closets, supply rooms, water heater closets, etc.)

Conference rooms

Interior office doors

Restroom doors

Exterior perimeter doors

Roof-top doors

Storm shelter doors

Fleet(s)/vehicle(s)

Fuel Pump(s)

Knox Box(es)

Take a look at most commercial building restrooms – there are locks on the toilet paper and seat cover dispensers. Point here is that keys are everywhere and not just the obvious places.

Starting with a blue-line print or floor plan of the floor/building/facility will help tremendously. Annotate the above locations on the plan with a specific identifier. It doesn't have to be complicated, a simple circled letter will do fine.

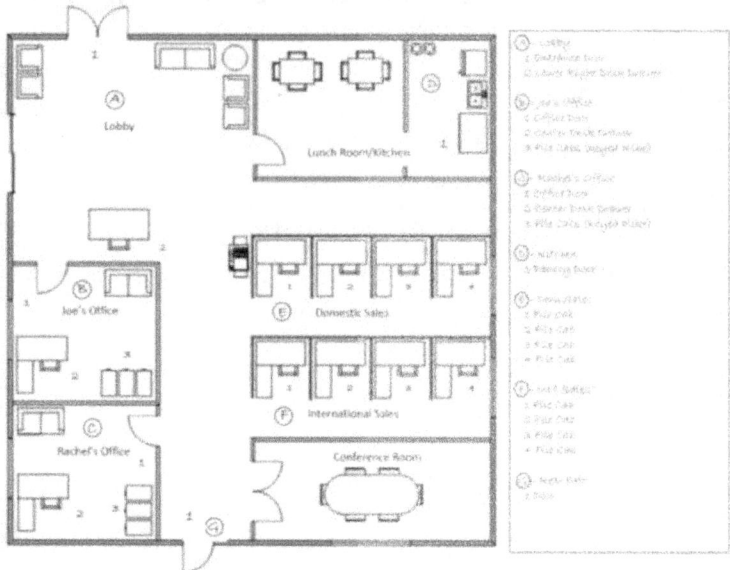

Assign a number to each lock next to your key list (example above).

Place the matching number on the floor plan or map of the building. The larger the facility, the more detail you'll need to have. Be as descriptive as you can as to the location of the lock you're identifying. This is not a process you want to go back and "do-over" because if you get it wrong, it may be a costly and time consuming fix.

I have found it helpful as I build my key control map, to color-code the map. In other words, using the example above, I would code the exterior access doors as YELLOW and private offices as BLUE, etc., I would then stamp the keys with a 'B' or a 'Y'. This coding is only known to and tied to the floor plan map. It allows lock & key managers and security managers to quickly identify a section or area a key belongs to just by glancing at it. You don't have to use color codes. Instead, you can use a series of numbers, where the first 2 or 3 digits reference (*to you*) a floor or a building while the next 2 or 3 digits tell you what type of lock, i.e. conference room, or private office or main access, etc. Point is – **Do not** mark keys with identifiers that someone can figure out easily.

To go off topic for a moment, but it applies I swear, I used to hold 1 hour "Brown Bag" lunch Security Awareness Talks for Office Staff and Administrative Assistants. One question I would ask is "How many of you are responsible for a petty cash box?" At least half or more would raise their hands. I would then ask those that were responsible for petty cash, "How many of you hide the Petty cash box?" Everyone would raise their hand. I continued, "How many of you hide the key to the petty cash box away from the box itself?" With proud faces, for doing the right security thing, they would all raise their hands. "Now," I would ask, "How many of you either hide your petty cash box in the lower right-hand drawer of your desk or in the bottom drawer of the file cabinet closest to your desk?" Eyes started widening with that question, "BUT, before you answer that question – how many of you, now tell the truth, hide the petty cash box key in the top 'pencil' drawer of your desk, hidden amongst the paper clips?" People are starting to laugh now, "with a little tag or piece of tape on the key, with the 'code' "PC" on it?" Everyone is giggling and looking around at each other. I would tell them that, believe it or not, the bad guys know that's where they hide the box and the key – and believe me, they can figure out what "PC" means. So…don't mark your keys with anything that can be easily figured out – it defeats the purpose of your goal.

Okay, back on topic -
Using a small manila key envelope, mark the envelope with the key/lock # and the number of individual keys for that lock and place all copies of that key inside the envelope.

Note: You're building this plan for others to be able to read and follow easily. There should be no room for question!

Who are you giving the keys to?

Now that you've got all of your keys and/or key sets marked, who are you planning to give them to? The answer likely falls into a number of categories:

Individual User – The person that needs access to their office, file cabinet and/or work desk. This may be your employee or an employee of a tenant in the building.

Regular Vendors – This would include the janitorial/custodial, security and maybe engineering staff, if that work is outsourced. On the janitorial or custodial side, these vendors usually require sub or floor masters to perform their services. Creating sub masters in a large facility significantly reduces risk of having to re-key a whole building if a key is lost. Most companies that fall into this category are well versed in key control. But that doesn't prevent them from losing keys!

An example of this would be a 50 story building. Instead of giving a janitor a key that accesses the whole building when they're only assigned to clean floors 4, 5 & 6, a "Floor Master" is created that only opens those floors. If the key is lost or misplaced, a locksmith would only need to re-pin the cores (of the locks) on the floors affected by that individual's lost key.

Limited On-going Vendors – This would apply to vendors that visit your facility often but not every day, such as elevator companies, landscape companies, interior plant services, pest control and window washers. Handing over a set of master keys to one of these vendors can be a very risky undertaking as most vendors in this category do not understand the significance of a master key. I recommend never doing it.

Temporary User – An individual user could also be a "one-time" user. For example, when there were TI's (tenant improvements) or construction going on in a building, we would need to issue keys (usually one or two) to the contractor or construction people on a short-term basis. They were required to check these keys in and out every day. It is usually this type of situation where the risk of not getting the key back is the greatest. We would never issue a master key and rarely a sub-master key to contractors. If there is new construction going on, then we issue Construction Masters. All locks are keyed alike and access is granted to the holder to only those areas under construction. This usually isn't a problem as the only "valuable" property in construction areas tends to belong to the construction company or their contractors. Additionally, it is most likely that the responsibility for a new construction project falls on the General Contractor. In other words, until the project is completed, inspected and a Certificate of Occupancy issued to the Owner or the Owner's Agent, the General Contractor indemnifies the Owner from any and (usually) all events or actions while the project is under their control.

Managers – This classification relates to a Manager of the property/facility owner. It could include their third-party property management company, which in that event would include employees like:

Portfolio Manager(s)

On-site property/facility manager

Chief Engineer

Leasing agents

Typically, On-site Managers and Chief Engineers are issued master keys. The Chief Engineer may even carry a Great Grand Master (GGM) – s/he is on-call 24/7, so they need to be sure that when they're called in, they have all the access they might need.

Tamper Proof Key Rings

Now that you know which user needs access to what keys, the next step is to put individual keys onto key rings. When dealing with master keys, it is important to know that they cannot be easily duplicated. I'm sure many of us have seen keys with the words "Do not duplicate" on them. But the sad reality is those words are practically meaningless. One can go to Home Depot and put any "Do not duplicate" key inside one of the new automated cutting machines and voila, out comes a duplicated master. I've even seen people put a piece of tape over the "Do not duplicate" stamp on a key, hand it over to a key maker at a local hardware store and the key maker duplicates it – no questions asked.

There are lock and key systems, such a Medeco® (an Assa Abloy Group company), which have extremely strong controls on the issuance of their key blanks. Only specially vetted, licensed locksmiths, which have signed a detailed key control agreement, are allowed to order Medeco® products and key blanks. They also manufacture lock cylinders that require special key cutting machines – Machines that Medeco® carefully controls. Medeco's® key blanks are specially "coined", like U.S. coins with the Medeco® name and the name of the locksmith they have authorized to cut keys with their blanks. This helps control unauthorized duplication of Medeco® keys. The downside to this type of system is that it can be quite costly to end-users.

Split Keyring

This is where I recommend using a tamper proof key ring to hold keys together. If you use the standard split keyring and only have Medeco® keys on it, the likelihood is that copies won't be made without someone going through a lot of pain and effort. However, if you place regular keys or card keys on a split keyring, the risk of keys being removed and possibly copied is very high.

Tamper proof keyrings, per se, didn't exist when I started in the business. I remember it being a requirement at shift change, that the on-coming officer had to count the number of keys that were on the keyring and log it into his/her Daily Activity Report (DAR). If the keyring had less keys than it was supposed to, the off-going officer had to explain why – and that wasn't a report any of us wanted to fill out. A few years later the maintenance department came up with the idea of soldering shut the split keyrings, which was nice because we didn't have to count the keys, only double check that the solder wasn't cracked or split.

The need for ensuring that critical keys stay on keyrings and that there is some kind of accountability from its users has made way for true tamper proof keyrings. The latest products available are made from plastic coated locking cables or individually serialized (numbered) stainless steel. These rings are crimped closed, usually with a special tool, and can only be "opened" by destroying the ring. Tamper proof keyrings come in all shapes and sizes. I highly recommend this type of product for any key control program. You can also add small color tags to your key ring to quickly identify which vendor group or building section the keys belong to.

Lucky Line
Locking Cable

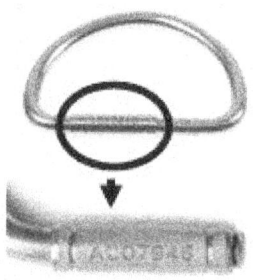

Cobra Serialized
Key Ring

Will the keys stay with the user?

Okay, so we've identified and marked the keys. We know what keys we have and how many we have. We know who's going to get them and what access they're going to need. Now – we're going to "sign out" a set of keys to them. How do we know or what incentive does the employee have to ensure that the keys we issue to them are going to stay with them at all times?

For example, someone who has been issued a set of keys is approached by their assistant that needs to put a few supplies in a closet. The assistant needs a specific key only for a few minutes so they can put the supplies away. The keys are handed over and the assistant, who instead of handing the keys back, simply places the keys on a nearby desk or counter and walks away. It can and *has* happened to all of us! Can you identify with "Holy Sh$% where are my keys? I swear I had them just a second ago!" Well this is heard more often than we want to admit. ***Keep reading*** – **Keys may never be lost again! I first got the idea in 1987 and then finally invented it in 2011.**

The Key to Keys

As a security guy, I've recommended different methods of carrying keys to my clients over the years. Unfortunately, there aren't many methods. People have been carrying keys the same way for decades. The most popular is a clip of some kind that attaches the key ring to your belt loop. I recall in the 1980's, when I worked security at a large resort, we had a big problem with Room Cleaners (called Maids, back then). They would leave their ring of keys on top of their Maid's cart outside of the room, while they were inside cleaning. This resort was on a 43-acre island. All of the rooms (or cottages, actually) were accessed from outside. In other words, it wasn't a high-rise type hotel building with long hallways of doors. As a result, someone, anyone, could walk by a cottage with a housekeeping cart in front of it and grab the keys from the top of the cart. The maid would never know (at least until the keys were needed again).

Missing keys from carts happened way more than we wanted to admit. When I first started working there, when keys were lost, the maintenance people would just cut new keys and build a new ring of keys. It was not long after that and a few big dollar lawsuits that had come through the court system (not involving the resort), that resort management made a major investment in one of the first "card key"-type locking systems. It was called CorKey. CorKey is not an electronic access system like you see today, as those didn't exist yet. It was a manual locking system that was operated by a metal or plastic card-type key, called PowerCards® and a series of magnets. I don't recall exactly how many but there was at least a combination of magnets situated amongst a ~100 or so magnet placement locations inside the lock. The key was a metal, oval disk, about the size of a business card – when the key was inserted into the top slot of the lock, all of the magnets in the knob had to line up with the combination of magnets in the key, you could then turn the knob and open the door.

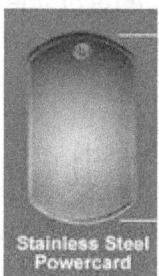

Plastic Powercard   Stainless Steel Powercard

If a key was not turned in after the guest checked-out, then security would go out to the room and change the combination of the magnets in the lock and two new keys would be made. It didn't take very long to do this. We had the ability to quickly change the placement of the magnets in the lock, but we were limited to only four total lock change combinations. It was done with a small little tool that was inserted in the lock and turned. It rotated a magnet wheel. After you had rotated the magnet wheel three times, you had to reset all of the magnets in the wheel, like re-pinning a core. Then you got four new lock combinations and three more quick changes for that lock.

This was one of the first lock and key systems I had seen that did not require rekeying of a lock or building in the event of a key loss. However, that said — we still had a risk. If someone snatched the maid's keys from the cart, they could start using it to enter other guest rooms, unbeknownst to anyone. I am happy to say that CorKey still exists today. Very little has changed with regard to their technology (that I can tell), but they have kept up with the different locking hardware requirements and configurations. They're worth looking at: http://www.CorKey/com.

Even with this new locking system, there was still too big of a risk with employees losing keys, especially when considering safety and security exposure to guests. In order to eliminate that risk, what we needed to do was to come up with a way of preventing the housekeeping staff from separating from their keys at all times. After much discussion, we created a long leather (round) belt with a loop on one end and a key ring on the other. There was also a leather "bell" that could slide along the belt and cover the keys so they wouldn't clang as the user walked around. It was expected that the housekeeping employee would wrap the leather belt around their waist, put the "key end" through the loop on the other end and let the keys lay against their side. Well that great idea lasted about a week until we started seeing leather bells hanging off the side of the carts.

Over my career, I've looked for and tried many different tethering solutions. There are key holders that easily slide on your belt or shirt pocket. Many have physical tethers, like string, chain, nylon, even Kevlar, that are attached to a spring loaded mechanism. If you pull the key out and let go, it retracts back into the holder. I tried really hard to deploy all of these; I wanted them to work – I really did. My security people used their keys many, many times per day. The string and chain solutions don't last very long. The retractable chain locks up and knots. We replaced those on a regular basis. The nylon tether has its wear limit as well. I've also heard a story where the chief engineer of a 50-story high-rise lost his keys when the Kevlar cord broke. He didn't realize it until an hour later. Fortunately for him, the keys were found by a tenant in the building who returned them to the management office.

Two other things I really don't like about the holder unit is that, one, the belt clip slides on and off the belt too easily – which allows the user to hand off his/her keys when someone else needs them. Two, some of the nylon and Kevlar units have extremely powerful reels and springs in them – so much so that I have had Workers' Comp claims filed, because our officer almost broke her finger when she let go of the key ring.

No matter how "fool proof" the system that we used for securing keys to the employee, I still got calls that someone has lost or misplaced keys. The inevitable conclusion is that once keys are in use by an employee, they're susceptible to loss. I continued to ponder that fact.

It was 1987. I was an Operations Manager with a national security company. Our branch had just been informed that we lost a set of master keys at a large high-rise building in downtown San Francisco. I was flabbergasted as I had implemented some pretty strict key control procedures at that location. I also knew that my crew was really careful about following protocol.

I don't know, to this day, what happened and how my officer lost the keys. I believe that the key ring must have fallen off his belt clip either in the restroom or somewhere outside the building. The first time he realized the keys were missing was when he tried to get back into the building after being out on a patrol.

Later that night, after convincing the client that we'd find the lost keys, my assistant and I went to a bar in the city to lament what just happened. It wasn't the first time. I remember Jim and I sat down with a cocktail and a bunch of napkins. We began to sketch out what we believed would eliminate lost keys forever. Could we really design something that would prevent a security officer from *ever* losing their keys?

I still have the design written down. The downside to that idea was that the technology we wanted to use didn't exist. We could've been talking about jet packs or driverless cars, for that matter – it wasn't going anywhere. But the good news is that we live in a world of rapidly changing technology.

What we needed, I felt, was some sort of key holder that would literally prevent our people from losing their keys. Something that was preemptive, not an "after-the-fact" solution, i.e. you've lost your keys and now you need to find them. Unfortunately, there was nothing I was aware of that would do that.

I've been searching for that missing link to the key control process for more than three decades. I attended all the national conferences where the latest technology was on display, virtually every year; ASIS (American Society for Industrial Security), ISC West (International Security Conference), BOMA (Building Owners and Managers Association), IFMA (Institute of Facility Management), ACA (American Correctional Association) and the IACLEA (International Association of Campus Law Enforcement Administrators). I kept looking for something that I could buy that would preempt on-shift key loss, but to no avail. I made it a habit of going up to the key cabinet vendors, asking to hear their sales pitch. And when they were done, I'd ask, *"And how does this fancy cabinet prevent my employees from losing their keys?"*

You may be aware of the electronic "key-finders" that are now on the market, that are tied to a smart phone with an app. I think these are great consumer solutions. If you can't find your car keys in your house somewhere, there are only so many places they could be. But I haven't seen one item finder yet that works in a commercial environment. And even if you are in range of your lost keys, the little beepy sound that most of them put off, at least to me, is essentially inaudible. Nope, what is needed here is something that is preemptive. Mine wouldn't be an "item finder", it would be an "item I can't lose in the first place" thingy...and if a user happens to put their keys down and starts to walk away, then they need to be alerted **Big Time**. I envisioned my device alerting every sense (except smell and taste – although I haven't licked it, actually) – no, I wanted them to know sensorally, by sound, feel and sight. I think my device has knocked it out of the park!

Have the keys been returned?

Now that you have i) identified the keys that you plan to issue; ii) secured those keys in a specific control box; iii) a system in place for issuing the keys, and iv) done your best to ensure that the keys will stay with the user. The next thing you need to know is did you get the keys back once the user was done? In a standard key control program, that means the person comes to a central control area, turns in their keys and in exchange, their name is checked off on a key control list. Or if they gave up their driver's license or set of personal car keys, then that item gets returned to them.

With some of the newer electronic key control cabinets, the user will be notified via email or text at a set time *prior* to the keys being required to be returned, as a reminder. In the event the keys are not returned, the manager of that user is notified. This allows someone to try to track the person down before they leave to retrieve the keys. There are other ways to "try and catch" people leaving a building with their keys. Some of my clients used an RFID technology, placing sensors at egress points around the building and an RFID tag placed on the key ring. If somebody passes one of the RFID sensors with the keys, an alarm is triggered and notification is sent to the person's manager or whomever, indicating that the keys had just left the building. Of course, the keys are now gone and someone needs to move quickly to find the person to get the keys back from them.

III. Evolution of Key Control Programs

Remember earlier in this book when I talked about working security at a large resort? Well, one of our jobs was to issue sets of keys to the Housekeeping staff; Maids, Housemen (*as they were called then*), Supervisors and even the Director and Assistant Director of Housekeeping, checked out their sets of keys from us. We would also issue key sets to the Maintenance Department employees. This was a routine/ritual that took place about 15 minutes before each shift.

The department managers would issue each employee a numbered tag. This numbered tag denoted the key set and access privileges that each employee would have for the day. The employee would walk over to the security office where they would stand in line at the "Key Window". Key Windows at all the hotels I worked at were located "behind the scenes" where guests couldn't see what was going on. When the employee reached the window, they would hand their Key Tag to the security officer who would reach over to a wooden key box mounted on the wall. There were many rings of keys hanging on brass cup hooks with a corresponding number above the hook. The officer would pull the key ring off the hook and replace it with the numbered Key Tag.

That "program" seemed to work well and I never thought there was anything one could do to improve it! Just like when I paid $750 for a 40-megabyte hard drive for my Tandy computer and knew, categorically, that I would never need anything larger than that – ever!

As with everything else, things continued to evolve. Hotel management felt it was taking too long for employees to get their keys. The Key Window was too far for them to walk to and then walk back to their supply closets to start work. So it was decided that security would go to the departments and issue keys right there when employees were checking in for their shifts. The Maintenance Department removed our wooden key box from the wall and installed heavy duty hinges to the two doors along with a hasp and lock. A heavy brass handle was then added to the top of the box. We were now "portable". The box probably weighed 30 pounds and was as unwieldy as all get-out. It measured about 24" in length (with the doors closed, close to 50" with them open) and carried about 60 sets of keys. The box was only 4" or 5" deep.

We had to create a work around when we transported the box, via electric golf/security cart, as the keys tended to fall off the brass cup hooks. It would take two of us to carry the box flat, doors up, to help and hope that the keys would not pop off the hooks. We also modified one of the carts with a wooden ledge in the back seat so we could lean the box up against it so the box was right-side up – we just couldn't stop the cart too quickly or the box would tumble over. Either way, we'd usually spend 5 minutes when we reached the department hanging the ones that fell off, back up. Other than that, I liked our issuing procedure. It seemed quick and effective. It also helped that for the most part, we were issuing the key sets to the same people every day. We knew them and when they didn't show up to turn in their keys, we knew where to find them.

As I moved on with my career, I tried rolling out this kind of program in many different facility environments. But I came to find out that in less intimate settings, it wouldn't work so well. In a commercial building, for example, when keys were issued, the recipient was required to sign their name, list their company and enter the time they received the keys. Half the time you couldn't read the person's signature so we added a line for them to print their name – again, it

The Key to Keys

was very difficult to try and discern who forgot to return the keys. Finding a way to incentivize someone to return their keys was paramount.

I'm old enough to remember gas stations chaining the bathroom key to a huge, heavy tool, to ensure no one walked off with it; it usually worked. Or a high school Hall Pass. If you were allowed to be in the hall during class, you better be carrying that tractor tire – yes, something that size would not likely be replicated or forged and the teacher was sure to get it back! We started doing something similar – If you want a set of keys you must surrender your Drivers' License or other "valuable" card. You bring the keys back; we'll give you your ID back. This worked quite well. Needless to say, we had to make significant modifications to the old wooden key box with brass cup hooks. We needed to place clips next to the key holder so we could attach the ID and not lose it.

I'll never forget the first specifically-designed key box I ever laid my eyes on. It was the early '80's. It was more like a real cabinet; a thing of beauty (to the security professional). This box was amazing. It was made of metal, very rugged. It had tempered glass doors so you could see the key sets all the time. It required a combination to open the door(s). It could hold so many keys. The key hooks were built into the cabinet. It even had larger sized "cubbies" to place odd-sized items in for safe keeping. This was intended to be the answer to controlling keys, so they wouldn't get lost. But I came to find out that all they really did was tell you who lost the keys (which was still an improvement, as at least now we had accountability back to the employee). People became cognizant that the keys they were being issued were being tracked by managers and they better not lose them. In most cases, employees got better at not losing their keys (at least not as often). The electronic key cabinet business continues to evolve. Some of their newer products are extremely sophisticated.

Key Control Cabinets

Key control cabinets come in many shapes and sizes. The first versions were quite simple and operated much like a safe. Once you opened the box, by key or combination, you had access to all keys inside. Many security operations, to this day, use these types of cabinets.

My focus here is on the electronic cabinet. The traditional way of mitigating key loss has been to create accountability (see the second story under Chapter V, entitled Other Headlines Worth Pondering, where $162,000 was spent on electronic cabinets after keys were lost). Typically, what happens when a key set is lost is the rush to upgrade to an electronic cabinet. They serve to limit access to keys so that you know where keys are at all times. And if a set of keys goes missing, there is clear responsibility as to who lost the keys. Many commercial buildings use electronic boxes so there can be no doubt as to which vendor lost the keys (and therefore must pay for the rekey). There are five primary manufacturers of these products that I am familiar with:

Morse Watchmans, Deister Electronics, Assa Abloy (Traka), CaptureTech and KEYpers. All of them offer electronic cabinets which limit access to the key boxes through key, PIN, combination, or biometric methods. The boxes only release the keys to the user accessing the box that s/he is authorized to remove. Many provide an imbedded-cabinet cam that captures video of all transactions. More importantly, the systems provide management with comprehensive reporting metrics and analytics, and text or email notifications in the event a key has not been returned, when expected.

Traka's (Assa Abloy) fob

The Key to Keys

There is one other technology improvement that really only one of these manufactures has employed in their design – RFID. Electronic key boxes all require some sort of key fob/ring that is attached to the key or keys to be held in the cabinet. The fob is essentially plugged into a hole or slot in the box, which registers to the system whether the key is there or not. When the key is in the box, it is "locked-in" to the slot until the proper combination, PIN or biometric input is recognized and automatically releases the "hold" on the fob, thus allowing the user to remove them from the box. For years, the key fobs contained what's known as a "Dallas Chip" or "iButton®". The Dallas chip is a metal contact, that when inserted into a hole or slot of the cabinet, would make contact or connection via metal-to-metal, thus closing the electronic loop. That technology has been around since the 80's and it's still very effective.

Traka's 'Silver Bullet' fob

Morse Watchmans' fob

The downside for key cabinet users, however, is that using the Dallas chip requires on-going preventative maintenance of the metal contacts. The metal on the key fob can get really dirty over a short period of time. Think about it – a security officer making rounds every half hour, on every shift, and in every environment. The stuff that gets stuck to the metal of the key fob is then, when turned in, transferred to the hole or slot inside the key cabinet. It doesn't take a lot for the metal-to-metal contact to become more like a dirt-to-metal contact, rendering the purpose of the "key control" ineffective.

Deister Electronics' proxSafe line of key management boxes and cabinets use an RFID key fob. It's connectivity in the hole or slot in the cabinet is made by radio frequency/proximity. There is not metal-to-metal contact required and therefore, no preventative maintenance required.

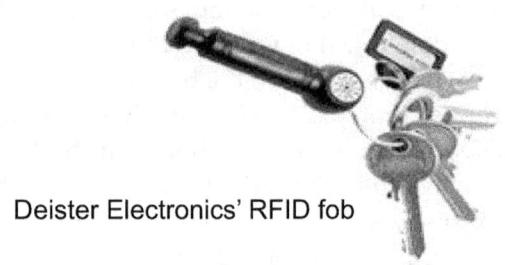

Deister Electronics' RFID fob

But they still do little to prevent the loss of keys when these keys are removed from the cabinet and go out on shift.

But hold on - now there is a way to prevent these key users from losing their keys – a device that is way overdue!

IV. True Stories

For more than 3 decades I was in a position that, if critical keys were lost or misplaced, I would get the call, usually in the wee hours of the morning, from a security supervisor or manager telling me, "Randy, we can't find our keys." What I really dreaded hearing, would come next, "We've all been looking for them for hours. What should we do?" What follows are three stories from literally a hundred or so that I have to choose from.

Story I –

One of my larger clients in Seattle was the owner of a Class 'A' commercial high-rise. It was a beautiful building with some pretty big name tenants. One of those tenants, at the time, was one of the largest U.S. banks. They occupied more than 80% of the building. The building was 42 stories and 900+ thousand square feet. It has a public plaza and several restaurants. There were also extremely secure floors, which required access through electronic turn-styles (those had just come out). We had separate uniformed security people monitoring the ingress and egress (which was quite a job, especially during the lunch hour). My company was providing ~1,400 hpw (hours per week) or 35 full-time security officers to that building. Our on-site Security Director was responsible for overseeing a 24x7 fire/life safety control room; visitor office, lobby console, loading dock access and foot patrol rovers.

It was a Sunday evening when I got the call. The Control Room officer had radioed one of the patrol rovers to the lobby to accompany a tenant that had left her office keys on her desk when she went on a dinner break. The Rover met the tenant and proceeded to the tenant floor. When they arrived at the office, the Rover reached to his side to unclip his key ring from his belt loop, he felt nothing – his keys were not there.

A supervisor was called and quickly responded to let the tenant into her office. The Rover and supervisor then spent the next 30 minutes retracing the Rover's steps. Based on the Rover's activity report, we could see that the last time he used his keys was three hours earlier. It was a weekend shift so things were a bit quiet, because the majority of the building was closed to the public. In that three-hour time span, the Rover had covered a lot of area; 8 levels of parking, the public plaza, the employees' lunch room, the lobby and almost 20 floors end-to-end. The Rover keys have everything on them; access cards, office masters (hard keys), utility closet/mechanical room keys, you name it. It was the Rover's job to respond to any area and be prepared to grant access if required.

In this case, the Rover had a separate key holder in his blazer pocket that held his primary access card. He still had that in his pocket. It was the full Rover key ring that was missing. By this time, everyone was looking for the keys. I sent Field Supervisors to the building who helped search. By about the 1-hour mark and no luck finding the key ring, I had no other choice but to call my client and tell her what has happened. Due to the risk of those keys getting into the wrong hands and the fact that a large banking institution (credit card transactions were being processed on several of the floors) could be breached, time was of the essence.

My client, Anne, was a Property Manager for an international commercial real estate company that owned the building. I can't repeat what she said after I told her a set of master keys were missing. We agreed to meet at the building right away. Anne's next step was to make a plan to notify her tenants. Mine was to get additional security personnel to the property so we could secure the building's perimeter. We needed to do this in case someone had found or stolen the keys and then tried to gain access to the building's many restricted areas.

For the next several hours, we were in a panic. Notifications were being made and the hunt went on but the keys could not be found. It was decided that the building had to be rekeyed immediately. The security risk was too high to wait any longer. Anne's Engineering department called in a locksmith so a new lock & key map could be built, the exterior perimeter rekeyed, as well as the "secure floors". The entire building rekey took 2 weeks and cost over $80,000. Guess who had to pay for the rekey? My company. You may be saying, 'Yeah, but Randy, that's why you have insurance.' Yes, but my company was self-insured for the first $250k. This is $80k that we will never see again and that amount did not include the extra security officers (many demanding time and a half) I had to add to the building during the rekey process...oh and I had to pay Anne for all of the engineering overtime and extra staff she had to put in place. All told, my final cost was in excess of $100,000.

Okay, *Ready for it*?

Two weeks after the rekey, we found the keys. They were on top of a soda machine in the break room, right where the Rover had left them. How we missed them after all that searching still haunts me to this day. But even if the keys were found a day or two later, we would have no idea if the keys had been taken, duplicated and put back where they were found – to eliminate this risk, the building would still would have had to be rekeyed.

Are you ready for it, again?

My client, Anne? I married her two years later! No, it had nothing to do with the fact that I could have lost that $1MM/year account...I mean, hardly anything to do with it.

Story II -

In a very up and coming business section of Seattle, known as South Lake Union, a set of janitorial keys were lost. It was just after 11:00 pm in a 6-story, 85k sq. ft. office building. I was notified by our client that she needed at least three security officers sent over right away. The Janitorial Company had already sent extra people down in an all-out search to find the missing keys. The security officers would be responsible for standing by the access doors to the building and identifying anyone wishing to enter. Authorized personnel would be carrying a photo ID/access card. Security would require they swipe their key at the card reader, confirm it turned "green" and the door opened or granted access.

The keyring that was lost had multiple hard keys on it that accessed virtually every office in the building, including the data center of an international, high-end clothing manufacturer. There were no card keys on it. Our client knew that she had to act quickly to placate a highly volatile and vocal building tenant representative.

We were able to staff the additional security within about 30 minutes. When we arrived, the janitorial staff was frantically searching for the missing keyring. In retracing steps, the janitorial supervisor was certain he last used the keys about 30 minutes prior to when he discovered the keys missing. He traced his steps from office floors into the lobby, to the janitors' storeroom and then into the loading dock area. He then realized he had to use his keys to access the janitor storeroom. From there, everyone focused on the trip from the janitor storeroom to the loading dock. Looking at the ground, the loading dock parking areas and driveway – EVERYWHERE! It was not a very large area.

By now about an hour and a half had passed. The janitorial supervisor is sitting next to the garbage and recycling dumpsters, racking his brain. He knew they had to be close – and then it hit him! He was carrying some large flattened cardboard boxes when he peeked inside at a schedule sitting on the desk in the janitor storeroom. He wasn't in there for more than 60 seconds. His keyring was in his hands when he came out. He walked directly to the dumpster and tossed the cardboard in...along with his keys! After a bit of dumpster diving, keys found – mystery solved. Fortunately for janitorial firm, the keys were lost in such a way that they could not have been found by someone else, copied and then put back. If you ask me, this was hugely lucky as it meant that our client would not require a $25k rekey. My company billed a 4-hour minimum for the three officers we sent down, which the janitorial firm was more than happy to pay.

Story III -

It's 6:00pm on a Thursday evening. Public access to this landmark building is now closed. One of the 4 swing-shift security officers, Officer Phillips, is issuing the Janitorial Supervisor the 12 sets of floor masters that her staff will need to clean the building until 2:00am. Believe it or not, the year is 2014 and the "key box" is literally a wooden box with ~20 sets of keys thrown in it. Janitorial services are provided by a service contractor, Sunday through Thursday.

The proper procedure for issuing keys is that the security officer would pull out one set of keys, identify the set number, log it out on the Key Sheet and then hand the set to the Janitorial Supervisor. The Supervisor would then confirm the set number and sign next to the entry the Security Officer made on the Key Sheet, verifying that she received the correct set of keys. In this case, however, that's not what happened. Instead, the Janitorial Supervisor dug through the key box, pulled out all of the sets she needed (like she does every night), looked at Officer Phillips at the desk and said, "Okay, I've got them all." Then Phillips says something like, "Great – have a good one!" He proceeds to write down the list of key set numbers that the Supervisor picks up every night (copying it from the previous day's list) and makes some sort of initials after the list.

The building is 50 stories, more than 800k sq. ft., with over one hundred tenants. The tenants range from a prominent law firm to a "classified" company that does secret research. That company's name isn't even listed on the building's tenant directory and access to their floors are highly monitored.

It is the end of the janitorial shift, 2:00am Friday morning. The Janitorial Supervisor is looking for Officer Phillips at the security desk. He is out on a call and unavailable for a few minutes. The Janitorial Supervisor wants to go home, so she radios security and says she's putting the key sets back in the box. Security says thanks and to have a good night.

It was a busy shift for security on that night. Bars in the area were closing and that made for a lot of intoxicated people walking around the exterior perimeter of the building. Some were knocking on the windows or sitting on the marble steps to smoke or continue drinking out of their own bottles. It wasn't until 4:00am that Officer Phillips returned to the lobby console. In addition to making all of his Daily Activity Report entries, he had an incident report to write. He finished those by 4:45 am – just in time to do patrol rounds of mechanical rooms and the building's exterior perimeter. 5:15 am rolls around and Phillips sees that he hasn't "inventoried" the janitorial keys yet. He looks in the key box, it appears to have all the sets of keys. He's been working with this Janitorial Supervisor for almost a year now and he's never had an issue, so he signs off on the key sheet that all key sets are accounted for.

Flash forward two days – it's Sunday afternoon and the janitors are returning to work after a few days off so they can make the building sparkle in time for tenants to return to their offices at 8:00am Monday morning. The Janitorial Supervisor goes to the Security Console desk to check out all her key sets. Officer Phillips is off on Sundays and Mondays, Officer Spencer is on duty and begins issuing the key sets, using the proper procedure. It doesn't take long for both Officer Spencer and the Janitorial Supervisor to realize that the Supervisor set of keys are not in the box.

After several hours of everyone looking for the keys, the Security Officer notifies his Account Manager and tells him what happened. The Account Manager calls the Branch Manager of his security company who in turn, calls the client at home, Sunday night, to tell her that we can't find a set of keys with masters on it. The client, understandably, is livid – It's Sunday night, the building re-opens tomorrow morning at 7:00am and she needs to notify her tenants that there's been a potential breach of the building and their space. Not good at all.

The client wants to know what happened. Her tenants are going to demand an explanation and a plan to re-secure the building, immediately. Security is pointing at Janitorial for losing the keys and Janitorial is pointing at Security for not logging them in when they were returned, two days earlier. Of course, the first priority is to secure the exterior perimeter doors into the building. While these doors and many of the interior doors have proximity card readers, they also have hard key locks, in the event there's a malfunction or other issue with the card access system.

Our client had locksmiths and additional engineers on the property first thing Monday morning. Extra security was added until the exterior locks could be re-cored. This was an older building so there were many lock sets/hardware that had to be changed out completely. Those locks did not have interchangeable cores. The rekey project lasted 9 days at a cost of $106k. Who paid for it, you might ask? Who was really at fault here, Security or Janitorial? Well, the client decided that we were each 50% culpable.

A lot of people ask, "Well, don't you have insurance to cover losses like that?" Many don't. In this case, the janitorial company was self-insured up to the first $250,000, so they paid $63,000 cash. My company had a $25,000 deductible, so we paid $25,000 with insurance picking up the rest (which I got to repay over time via increased premiums). This is cold, hard cash that neither company will ever see again. They will not recoup that loss from profits of that job for many, many years. What's more, both companies risk having their contracts terminated by the client for being negligent. Billing, for both companies, ranged from $30,000 to $55,000 per month – an account you don't want to lose. But guess what else that particular client has? Two other properties that are also serviced by both the janitorial and security contractors – if you lose one, the likelihood is that the client will take all of their services out to bid.

Scary what the impact of one stupid mistake, not following procedures or accidentally losing a set of keys, could have. The breach from when the keys went missing to when it was discovered that they were lost, was **72 hours**! To this day, we don't know what happened to the Janitorial Supervisor's keys on that Thursday night.

V. Other Headlines Worth Pondering

Seldom do key loss stories make print. When they happen, all we want is to sweep them under the rug. We want them go away quietly. Fortunately for me, none of my true stories above made headlines. However, here are a few others that did.

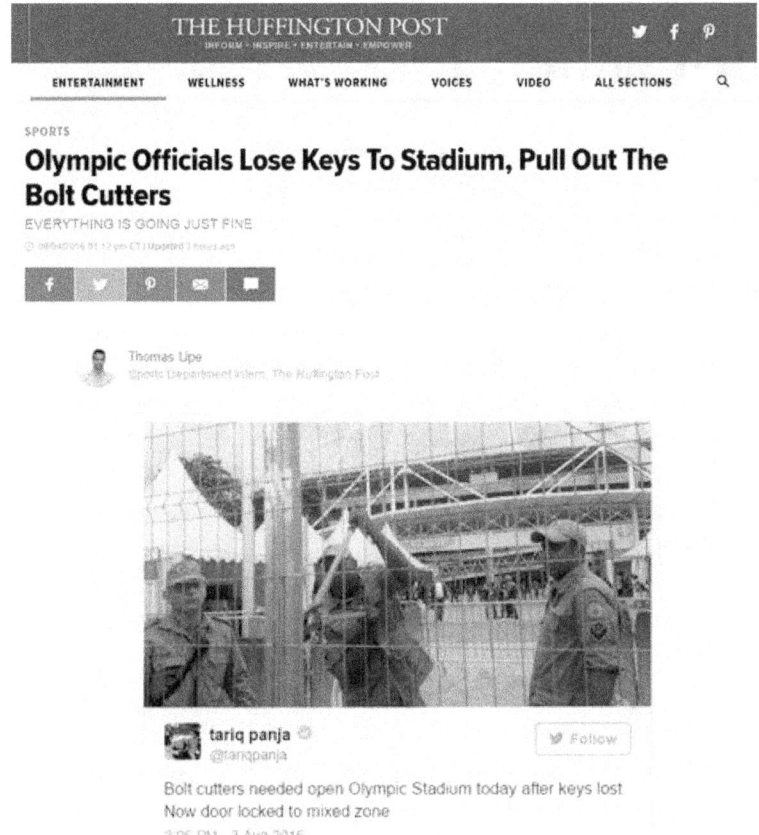

Randy Neely

The Rio Olympics did not get off to a smooth start.
Though the Opening Ceremonies for the 2016 Olympics will be held Friday, the games began Wednesday with the group stage for women's soccer. However, Rio officials did not seem to be very well-prepared, apparently losing the keys to one of the Olympic Stadium's two gates.

According to BBC reporter Julia Carneiro, the key for the east gate had been misplaced, forcing fans to line up for two hours before being sent to another entrance.

It was not disclosed by officials whether the lost keys were ever found.

January 29 of 2016, the headline read:

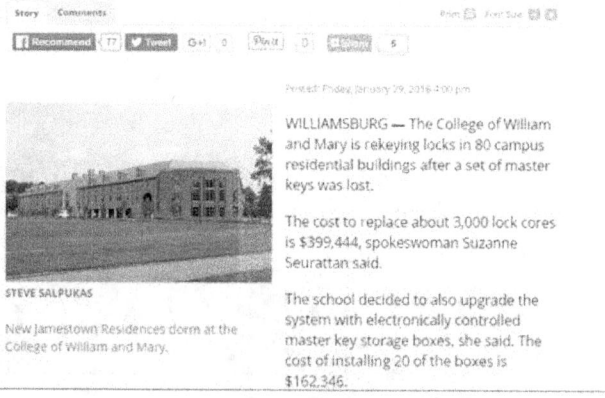

The Key to Keys

It was announced that in the Fall of 2015, the College of William and Mary, the second oldest U.S. college, was unable to account for a set of master keys. Keys that opened all of the campus' residential buildings (except for one), which included:

15 on campus Freshman Halls,

26 Upper Level Halls,

Graduate Residence Complex consisting of 9 buildings and *ALL* Greek Sorority and Fraternity Houses.

Can you imagine the liability, should something have happened? The facilities staff began replacing lock cores, where able, or replacing hardware and locks, as there may have been hardware so old, they couldn't be retrofitted. The project includes replacing more than 3,000 lock sets that were not only securing residential buildings, but individual dorm rooms. It has been said that the replacement of the locks/cores will cost $399,444. They are also installing 20 electronic key boxes to help manage and control all of the keys...at the tune of $162,346. This project will likely require they rethink and build a new lock & key map. Some of the points to consider: *How many master keys will they need? How many sub masters? What about individual keys to single locks or doors?* This is a massive undertaking and time is of the essence – they need to move quickly, for obvious reasons.

The College Administration and Chief of Police stated that the safety of students is the priority during this rekey project and that the contractors working with the Facilities staff are properly licensed, insured and vetted. It is standard practice that those working on critical locks are escorted by security personnel.

As part of the re-coring, all old keys and lock cores will be turned over to the William and Mary, while student residents are expected to return their old keys in exchange for their new ones. The old keys and cores will not be re-used by the college, but are likely to be sold as surplus, at which point they could be repurposed by another organization or simply recycled for scrap metal.

Unfortunately, I recently learned that the Facilities Management for the college had decided not to invest in a solution to mitigate any potential future employee key loss, that key tracking and accountability will suffice for them.

Home » News » Local

Man arrested for burglary with master key at apartment complex where he lives

Thu, 04/02/2015 - 2:17pm | Mary Schenk

URBANA — An Urbana man suspected of using a master electronic key to enter an apartment in his own complex has been charged with residential burglary....

In his apartment they found the electronic master key, as well as an iPod that had been taken in the burglary discovered Sunday in that same complex.

Assistant State's Attorney Troy Lozar said the electronic master key had been missing about a month....

The Key to Keys

I really wanted to be sure I shared the above article with you. Earlier I talked about some misconceptions about cardkeys. I have heard many times, even from security professionals, that once a facility goes to electronic access, there's no need to go to great lengths (or any for that matter) in ensuring people don't lose their keys, because you'll never have to rekey a building. All you have to do is deactivate the cardkey. In this example, a card key was either found or stolen from a user. The user obviously didn't know and the burglar started using it. Lesson? If you lose a cardkey, there's still a breach that can have negative consequences. Be sure your employees don't lose or misplace their keys – ANY kind of keys!

Randy Neely

It was estimated that the rekey of Wembley Stadium would exceed £40,000 or $57,000 USD. Guess what – This was completely avoidable – Read on!

The Key to Keys

Randy Neely

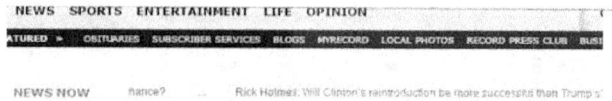

Lost key will cost district $15K to $20K

Lodi Unified forced to update locks at Bear Creek for second time this year

STOCKTON - A Bear Creek High campus supervisor has lost a master key, forcing the Lodi Unified School District to once again re-key all the locks, officials confirmed.

By Keith Reid

Posted Oct. 22, 2011 at 12:01 AM

STOCKTON - A Bear Creek High campus supervisor has lost a master key, forcing the Lodi Unified School District to once again re-key all the locks, officials confirmed.

The cost: between $15,000 and $20,000.

It is the second time in less than a year that Bear Creek has had to re-key the school's locks. Last October, former Principal Daryl Camp lost his master key at the high school, drawing criticism from staff members in an article published in the high school paper, The Bruin Voice.

The latest incident also has rattled school district leaders. Combined with the 2010 re-keying costs, the school district will spend at least $30,000 on locksmiths in 12 months at just the one school.

"I'm very upset about it," said Board of Trustee President George Neely. "It's getting ridiculous, and we're going to be looking at our procedures about this and for people that have these keys."

VI. Macro View of Users *(Snap Shot of User Silos)*

As you ponder the stories in the prior two chapters, the importance of a solid key control program becomes quite clear. Eliminating the security risk from lost keys is paramount in so many industries and environments. Below is a snap shot of some of those silos. I hope it will put into perspective for you how critical it is for the entire industry to recognize the risk associated with master key loss. It's time to stop the hush, hush. Everyone has an expectation that where they live, work, do business or are just visiting, the security of the building is sound. The people that have full access are supposed to make sure that they are not the cause of a breach.

Commercial buildings –

When you think about it, it's amazing how many industries are required to use and issue sets of master or sub master keys. One of the larger markets that I provided security services to is the Class-A multi-tenant office buildings. Some buildings had over one hundred tenants. And some of those had very "high risk" tenants; from top-tier law firms to government offices to high tech companies. Essentially a commercial high-rise is a city standing on its end with a population of thousands. From the standpoint of securing that kind of building, the exterior perimeter doors are the most vulnerable. Now-a-days, janitorial staff and their supervisors typically carry a floor master or multiple floor masters. These sets of keys open everything within their area of responsibility. Engineers of the building also carry masters and in some cases, grand master keys, so they could have access anywhere on the property at any time. Security people typically carry keys that grant them access to all parts of the building, as they are considered First Responders in many cases and must have immediate access in the event of a fire or other life safety issue.

Exposure in the event a set of master keys goes missing is significant. In the U.S. alone, where there are 5.6 million[1] commercial buildings, it is estimated that each building averages 2.7 master key sets, which means that there are ~14.9 million master key sets in use today! *Whoa!*

Building size range (sq. ft.)	1k-25k	25k-100k	100k-500k	500k-1M+	TOTAL BUILDINGS
No. of buildings	4,928,000	537,600	128,800	5,600	5,600,000
Workers with master keys					
Engineering	0	0-1	1-5	4-10	
Janitorial	0-1	1-4	4-10	8-25	
Security	0-1	1-2	2-8	6-24	
Management	1	1	2	2-3	
Avg. set(s) of keys per building	2	5	17	30	2.7

[1] - Source: US Energy Information Administration, 2012 Commercial Buildings Energy Consumption Survey.

Colleges & Universities –

You can imagine the number of college and university dorms or residential apartment complexes out there. This is another market where a loss of keys could have a devastating impact. In addition to the residents, keys are used regularly by facilities people, security and maintenance/engineering staff. Large residential buildings, large apartment complexes, as well as colleges and universities with residential buildings are high risk.

In order to eliminate the risk of key loss, many residential apartment complexes simply do not use master keys. Instead, they have a large cabinet where individual unit keys are locked away and stored. Apartments can get away with not having master keys, as there is no janitorial service and seldom is security provided. There is nobody who needs access to individual units on a regular basis. Maintenance workers are either let in by the apartment resident or check out the individual unit key from the manager, if so authorized, by the resident.

On the other hand, colleges and universities experience way more risk. Because most of them do use master keys, key management and liability challenges are abundant. Issues include compliance with federal legislation, such as Title IX, SaVE, VAWA and the Clery Act with its required Annual Security Report (ASR). Perhaps one of the greatest compliance risks colleges and universities face are legal in nature (Mullins vs. Pine Manor College and Peterson vs. San Francisco Community College). These cases found that colleges "…were obliged to take reasonable protective measures to ensure [student] safety against violent attacks and otherwise protect [them] from foreseeable criminal conduct and/or to warn [them] as to the location of prior violent assaults in the vicinity…". There are also reputational implications resulting from improper operational control over critical physical and electronic access keys and the potential harm to a student and/or employee resulting from a lost key.

There are a number of people that work within colleges and university facilities. People that carry critical keys and have access to residential areas, naturally create a high risk. If any of those keys are lost or misplaced, it places the safety of the students in jeopardy. Another example of this can be found in this book under Other Stories Worth Pondering, where a burglar used a stolen key at an apartment complex, to burglarize one of the units. You'll also see a headline that came out recently about a large and old college in the United States that is in the process of investing $460,000 in rekeying and installing a new key control program. They are rekeying thousands of doors and locks throughout the campus because one of their sets of keys went unaccounted for. The residential facilities in this college also include multiple buildings housing sororities and fraternities.

The college did not explain who lost the keys or what department lost the keys, they merely stated there was a ring of keys unaccounted for. Part of the rekey project included installing electronic key control cabinets. Many of the doors and hardware in some of those buildings were so old they were not able to replace the cores or re-pin locks, so new hardware and lock sets were required. Once they have completed this project they will have a significant key control program, but there's only one piece of this $460,000 key control program they will *not* have - ensuring that the users of the keys don't lose them, which is likely how the keys went "unaccounted for" in the first place.

Healthcare –

I think we can all agree that the healthcare industry is another market very vulnerable when it comes to key loss. One of my former client's building in the Pacific Northwest houses one of the largest regional pharmacies, the medical examiner's office, and a courthouse for the mentally disabled. In addition to the building employing locking mechanisms that are biometric and cypher-type locks, there is card access and hard key requirements throughout the facility. The loss of any form of access runs the risk of a severe breach that could affect many people. Think about the keys to a regional pharmacy going missing!

These types of facilities typically have some proper key control protocols, but one thing many of them don't have is a way to ensure that those people carrying these critical keys don't lose them. **Have I mentioned that I have the answer to this problem? I'm going to talk about that answer in just a little bit.**

Government buildings –

Government facilities – Did you know that the U.S. Government is the nation's largest landlord? In 2011, the New York Times reported that the government owns or manages more than 900,000 buildings or other structures - from office buildings, courthouses to warehouses and other property types. This is a "vertical" where lost keys could potentially have a global effect if keys are lost and found in the hands of the *wrong* people. The U.S. Postal Service, for many years now, gives all of their postal carriers' long chains that are attached to their key sets and those chains are attached to their belt and do not slide off their belt. They're literally slid onto the belt through a closed loop. If used properly, keys shouldn't get lost, however, there are stories about the chains breaking or getting caught on foreign objects. Yes, keys have been lost, but I would venture to guess not as often as those markets where the key sets can be easily pulled off the belt.

The problem is, in some cases, the carrier doesn't even know they're gone. Losing just one key from the "right" carrier could give someone access to hundreds of secured mailboxes. The U.S. Postal Service has taken steps to protect those keys even though the procedure in place is somewhat impractical, is a potential safety hazard, and still does not entirely prevent key loss.

There are other offices and facilities that belong to the government market where the government entity occupies space in public buildings, such as the FBI. There are FBI field offices that operate in leased space of commercial buildings all over America. While the security surrounding their floors or their office area is much greater in terms of physical barriers, allowing people in and out, keys are still required to get access to a building.

Obviously, the FBI takes special care of who they allow to have keys to access their facility and offices. However, as I'm sure everybody has in the past, agents have placed their keys down on a desk and walked away, forgetting they were there. It's an accident, but it happens. It happens to all of us at one time or another.

Hospitality –

Today, most hotels and some motels have key control down with regard to individual room keys. Typically, the keys that are issued to the guest do not have the room number on it so if they're lost someone won't know exactly what they have. Employees working in the hotel, however, have both access cards and hard keys that access many restricted areas of the hotel like mechanical rooms, back-end departments like housekeeping, maintenance and the back room of the Front Desk. There is still an issue, as not everything an employee has access to is programmed onto their cardkey.

You'll find that many employees also have hard keys on their rings. These could access accounting, the GM's office, the Gift Shop, and more. A lot of hotel employees are given a choice to wear a lanyard with the cardkey (and usually only a couple of other keys). The idea of a lanyard, from the standpoint of deterring an employee from setting it down and walking away from their keys, is a good one…but it still happens. Sometimes the employee gets tired of the lanyard being too long or too short and just puts it in their pocket. **This is a different method of carrying keys – but I have the answer to this one too!**

Depts. of Corrections –

Can you imagine the high risk in a jail or prison environment? If a key is lost or misplaced, the repercussions could be significant. A few years ago, I saw an airing on MSNBC's LOCKDOWN where it was discovered that the Armory key to the Maricopa County Jail was missing. Jail administration had hoped the missing key was accidentally taken home by an Officer, but after many phone calls, no one seemed to

The Key to Keys

know where it was. Because the key could be in the possession of an inmate, the entire facility must be searched. Shortly after the search commenced, more bad news came. It is believed that the missing key ring also has restroom keys on it. This means that a nurse, clergy volunteer or other civilian could have had the ring and perhaps taken it home and perhaps even made a duplicate key.

Apparently the lost keys mysteriously reappeared on someone's desk – an area that was already checked during their initial search. They could have been left behind somewhere or taken home by accident and that person didn't want to own up to it, so they just brought them back.

"I've misplaced my keys to the Kingdom."

VII. Components of a Successful Key Control Program

We've looked at "key control" of the past. When a master or sub master key was lost at a hotel (or an individual room key, for that matter), the Maintenance Department cut a new one. Interchangeable cores didn't really exist back then, and those that did were cost prohibitive. Hotel/Building/Facility owners and managers cannot take such risks anymore.

Courts have been clear that these owners, managers, contractors, service providers, etc., have a duty to the safety and security of their guests, employees, visitors and anyone else that happens upon their property. We've also read about some pretty scary True Stories and understand that effective key control programs and protocols are needed in virtually every environment, business and industry.

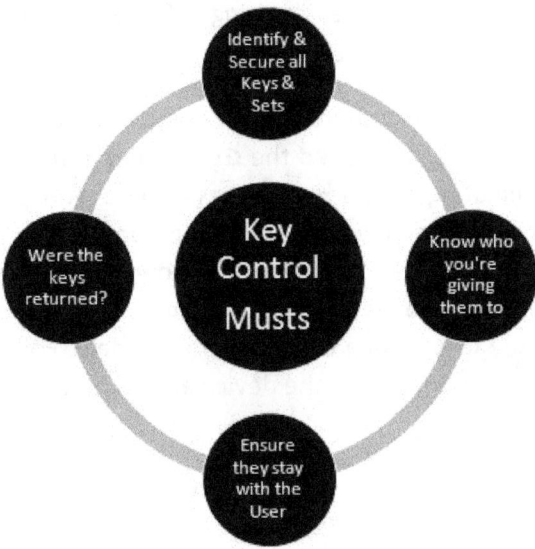

- ✓ Know what keys you have. Identify/Mark your keys. Have a secure place to store them and use tamper-proof key rings.
- ✓ Know exactly who you're issuing the keys to, and create an incentive for the user to return the keys.
- ✓ Know when keys are supposed to be returned and document the return. Build in contingencies for when the return time passes.
- ✓ Use a carrier or holder that you know will stay with the user. Take steps to ensure the user doesn't accidently hand the keys off to someone else or lay them down and forget about them.
- ✓ Use a device that prevents the user from losing their keys

The first four checks were policies and procedures that I had followed for years, but my employees still kept losing keys. It was driving me nuts. After years of hearing me complain, Anne, my wife and former client in **True Story I**, had also had enough. I kept saying to her, "If only there were some kind of a device that would alarm when keys were left behind." She told me that she's been listening to me talk about this idea for years, every time there was a near-loss or an actual loss of a client's keys. It was time to "get off the pot" so-to-speak and make it happen. The frustration I've felt trying to find a solution to this issue had finally reached its boiling point.

And to make a long story short, that's when I invented the electronic key tether, or **ekt**®, now called the *Gravity* Key Tether. My life-long fantasy of eliminating master key loss has finally become a reality! You can read more about how this invention came to be in the next chapter. But for now, all you need to know is that *Gravity* is the solution that you too have been looking for; the first and only preemptive key loss device on the market today. Following is our *Gravity* Fact Sheet describing the device and its benefits.

The Key to Keys

FACT SHEET

The New Force of Certainty in Key Control

Tether Technologies' GRAVITY is the first and only industrial-grade, digital tethering solution that automatically preempts master key separation and loss - with absolute reliability. Now you can rest assured of never having to experience a card/key loss event and its costly aftermath.

Never Risk Losing Master Keys or Access Cards Again

GRAVITY doesn't find access cards/keys, because they are never lost in the first place. GRAVITY tethers your cards/keys by using an electronic signal that works as a 5-7 step, mobile barrier around the worker. Upon breaching this radius, GRAVITY's unique alarm, vibration and strobe light are triggered.

Top Features & Benefits

- **Preemptive:** As workers do their job, GRAVITY does its magic ensuring cards/keys are always kept close at hand.
- **Ease-of-Use:** Press on the key unit's thumb release button and return it to the belt unit with a simple click and snap.

INSIDE GRAVITY

Invented by Industry Veteran
GRAVITY was created by Randy Neely, a security industry veteran who saw first-hand the pain caused by losing master keys. After exploring all the key control systems on the market, Randy set out to solve the problem in a unique way - to never lose keys in the first place.

Assembled in the USA
GRAVITY is assembled in Washington State with only the belt clips and casings sourced overseas.

- **Three Way Separation Alarm:** When keys separate, the alert is instant and fool-proof. Belt and key units emit unique alarms based on feel (vibration of belt unit), audio (chirp and louder 85 dB alarm on key unit), and visual (strobe on key unit).
- **Industrial-Grade Quality:** GRAVITY is designed for industrial environments with usability in mind. The vibration feature can be felt through heavy utility belts and the 85 dB audio alarm can be heard in loud environments. GRAVITY runs on standard AAA batteries with an average life of six months. Once batteries reach 20% capacity, a warning chirp alerts users that they need to be replaced.
- **Scalability:** Multiple GRAVITY units can work in close proximity to one another because each key unit is uniquely married to its belt unit via an RF signal generator.
- **Storability:** The key unit can be un-paired from the belt unit and placed in a low-power state for off-shift storage within an access control cabinet. Removal from storage without re-holster to a belt unit causes alarm.
- **ROI:** Prevent even one temporary key loss event from happening and GRAVITY has paid for itself.

Don't be Confused –

In the past few years, there have been at least a half a dozen "Item Finder" products that have come on the market. They usually work with a Phone App and a BLE (low energy Bluetooth) connection. These are "after-the-fact" products. In other words, you've already lost the keys and now you want to find them. There are basically two types of operational modes for Item Finders, Passive and Active.

Generally, Item Finders work best in "Passive Mode." You realize your item is missing and then hope you are still in range when you set out to find it. When your car is in the garage and you can't find the keys, you know they must be somewhere in the house. Walking around room-to-room with smart-phone in hand, you're bound to come across your keys. After-the fact finders, as I call them, work okay as consumer applications. But imagine trying to find a set of lost keys inside of a 240-acre college campus, especially when it's been hours since you last remember that you had them. In this case, the Item Finder has already failed as you have a potential security breach in play.

Some Item Finders allow you to put them in "Leash" or "Active" mode. But here they have proven to fail miserably as constant false alarming irritates the user to the point where they either stop using the Item Finder completely or switch it back to Passive mode. **Gravity** is Leash mode on steroids. It uses a local two-way radio system, kind of like a set of "Walkie Talkies". **Gravity** also uses BLE, but in a much different way. With its AAA batteries, **Gravity** powers up the BLE signal in a way that Item Finders can't. **Gravity's** belt and key units, when together, are off (near zero power draw) and when separated, are in constant communication. The moment the signal drops below a certain threshold (i.e., distance of separation), both units cry out, alerting the user instantly that they've stepped too far away from the other. You just can't lose your keys, period!

Looking forward with the **Gravity** and other Tether Tech products –

With the technology we've included in the current version of the **Gravity**, we now have, for all intents and purposes, a battery-powered computer chip on the belt of the User. In the near future, we will be able to measure User productivity and/or log when keys are used and when the device alarms. These are metrics that management will be able to call up and view in real-time or historically. Users will have the ability to customize their unit; adjust the alarming distance, change the volume of the alarm(s), the pitch or sound of the alarm and even increase the intensity of the vibration on the belt. We have been testing and adding different ways of attaching the **Gravity** to the User. Envision a Smart Belt Tether that would allow you to attach virtually anything to it without a separate belt unit – the entire belt hosts any device you attach to your belt or person, for that matter. It's right around the corner.

The way in which people have carried keys hasn't changed in many, many decades and the frequency of people losing keys hasn't changed either. Remember not too long ago, when someone thought of adding wheels to a suitcase? Wow! That, like the **Gravity**, is becoming the **new** standard.

If you are saying to yourself, "But Randy, I don't lose keys" – that's probably true. Over my entire career, I can only remember losing a set of keys once or twice. And that was only for about 5 minutes or so. But as I got promoted into management, that's where the problems really started for me. It was my responsibility for others, particularly entry level personnel, together with the law of large numbers that is when key loss becomes inevitable. In fact, I'm certain that I didn't even hear about most key loss incidents. That's a disciplinary offense, so what do most employees do? That's right; search first, maybe even for an hour or two, and hopefully find the lost keys. And if not, that's when they finally report them as missing.

Are you considering replacing your hard keys with an electronic access card system? Are you doing that because you don't want to face the consequences of lost keys? Remember, access cards only save you from the costly rekey. In 99% of lost key cases, keys are found, but the security breach remains. **Gravity** offers an alternative solution that will save you a ton of money and time, but more importantly, total elimination of any potential security breach.

So what if you are currently using an electronic cabinet to store and account for keys? Then **Gravity** is absolutely for you. I believe that by incorporating **Gravity** into your electronic key control cabinet – you will have a fully-rounded key control program. The key cabinet creates accountability, letting you know who checked out which set of keys and if those keys don't make it back to the box. **Gravity** ensures that checked out keys don't get lost when they are out on shift. Imagine that - **a world with zero key loss** - a facility manager's dream.

Here ends the main focus of my book, a discussion of keys, key control and various ways to mitigate key loss. You understand *why* I invented **Gravity**. Now if you want to learn more about *how* I invented **Gravity**, then I invite you to keep reading.

PART II

VIII. Inventing the Solution

Okay, here's how the rubber hit the road. This is the solution I was drawing on a piece of paper in 1987, but the technology didn't exist. I wanted to create something that was preemptive, something that would prevent my security officers from losing their keys in the first place. If they left their keys behind, it had to alert them. Not only did the keys have to grab their attention, but I wanted their body to "tap them on the shoulder" as well.

It had to be super easy to use. Otherwise, re-training and sabotage would cause failure. It had to resemble the action(s) of something they're used to already. It needed to be durable. Any of you ever get calls or hear about two-way radios falling in the toilet or down an elevator shaft? I could write pages on all the "stories" of how a piece of my employee's equipment was damaged or lost. It was not unusual to hear about a string of "misfortunes" with my staff, especially when we introduced new tools for them to use. Tour wands are a prime example. I can't tell you how many "lost" wands I've had to replace over my career.

For many, many years, our industry used "Watch Clocks" to prove that rounds were being done. Two of the most popular Watch clocks were put out by Detex and Morse. These clock systems were pretty straight forward. We would strategically hang keys (on chains) in little weather resistant key boxes, around the property. We'd pick areas of the property that we really wanted to be sure security was checking all the time, such as mechanical rooms, exterior storage facilities, roof hatches. Then we'd put up temporary "stations" when we were having issues in a particular location. Anyway, the security officer would hang the clock across their chest (using a strap) and make their rounds, pulling the keys out of box and inserting them into the clock and turning the key. The clock would then time stamp when they were there.

The concept was great and it worked well. In many cases, we needed the record to prove to insurance companies that we were checking hazardous areas on the property or heat temperatures on mechanical equipment. But like everything else, there were always "those" employees that didn't like using the clock. You see, the employees did not have the special key that opened the back of the clock where the tracking disc or tape was recording their activity, otherwise they'd find a way to "fix" the rounds. I can't tell you how many times I would get reports that keys were missing or the clock (later clocks were made out of a hard plastic) was damaged or broken and no one knew how it happened.

I apologize for the tangent, but it's important to know that trying to change one's behavior, in particular their routine, can be a challenge. You have to be ready for push-back.

Okay, back to this big solution! I am not an electrical or mechanical engineer nor did I know how to invent something, let alone bring something to market. Frankly, my intention was not about bringing anything to market. All I wanted to do is come up with something that would stop my people from losing their damn keys! I am going to spare you the long, and I mean long, story of how all the pieces came together. It has been a long but incredibly amazing experience. So here's the "Reader's Digest" version:

It was mid-2005, three years after **True Story I** and my $100,000 fiasco. Craigslist was new, certainly new to me. After speaking with a patent attorney, I was told I needed more than a hand-drawn sketch (Fig. 1) to prepare a patent application. I had to clearly describe the operation details of my invention and articulate (in an Abstract) what makes it novel. Okay, not sure how to do that, so I shared my idea with a few close friends. They suggested I put an Ad on Craigslist, looking for an electrical engineer for a short project I was working on. Within 3 days, I had a few responses and one in particular stuck out. It was from a recent graduate from Washington State University. Best part was that he didn't live too far from me. We arranged to meet at a coffee shop so I could explain the project.

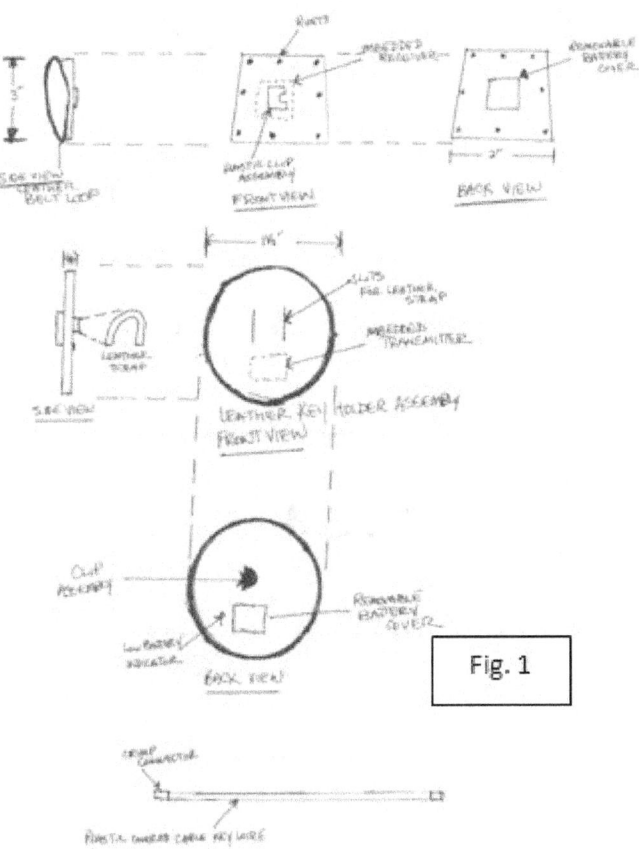

Fig. 1

After agreeing to sign a Non-Disclosure Agreement, I explained to Marc that I wanted to create a device that would prevent someone that is carrying a ring of many keys from losing them. I didn't want something that helped the user find lost keys. I wanted them to not lose keys in the first place. We spent a good hour and a half talking about the effected environments and the types of users. I wanted it dummy proof. It was Marc's job to precision-question me and to envision a formula on how and if something like this could even work. A week or two went by and Marc called saying he wanted to meet to give me an update.

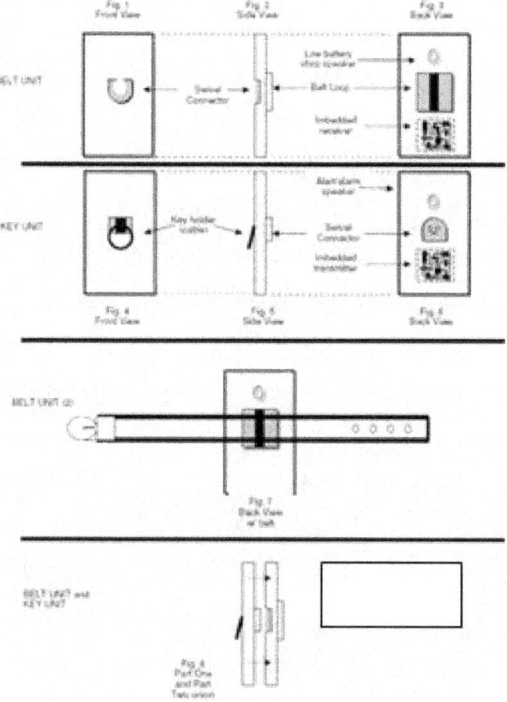

Fig. 2

The Key to Keys

We met again at the coffee shop and in his hands was to be the basic recipe for a solution I'd been dreaming of for so many years. As I looked at this engineering language and the attached bulleted description, Marc explained what it all meant. I was impressed. While I believed everything Marc was saying and tried to understand it, I kept thinking to myself what I'd need to do next.

What had to happen before I would have this device in my hand? I figured all I would have to do is go back to the patent attorney, show him my new computer designed (in Microsoft Paint) sketch (Fig. 2) of the device along with Marc's and my "formula" and get a patent. From there, I guess I would take the same information to an invention building company and have them make a prototype so I could mass produce them, deploy them to all my accounts and *Voila* – no more lost keys. **Wow** – Imagine that! Finally!

A few months later, I contacted the patent attorney I had met earlier in the year. I had given him a retainer to advise me on the steps I needed to take. I returned with the latest drawing/sketch and the formula. The attorney did a search for like or similar patents and returned a few that were somewhat similar, in terms of what they were intended to do. But my device operated differently enough and from a design perspective, mine was very unique. I needed a prototype, a proof of concept. Would this idea even work?

It would be another 3 years **and** another key loss event involving my security people, before my passion for this solution reignited. This time I had a serious conversation with my wife about this project. She completely understood the problem and agreed; she's never seen a solution after all her years in retail and commercial property management. Remember? Anne was my client in **True Story I**. She has felt the pain as someone that has been in a position to have to call the owner of the building and every tenant in the building, telling them that there's been a serious breach. As a result, she and her company ran the risk of losing the management contract for the building. She has seen the pain that I have experienced as a contract service provider. The frustration I've felt trying to find a solution to this issue had finally reached its boiling point.

I told her I was willing to commit the time and money to make this become a reality, but I knew it was going to be a long road and a very expensive undertaking. It was not something I was going to do without her 110% buy-in. She told me that she'd been listening to me talk about this idea for years, every time there was a near-loss or an actual loss of client keys, so it was time to "get off the pot" so-to-speak and make it happen. I had her commitment.

We're cook'in with oil now, baby!

It was July of 2009, a beautiful summer day on Vashon Island. We invited a couple over to the house for the weekend. Crab season was in full swing and we had plenty of butter! As Dennis and I sat on the deck, we started talking about better ways of shelling a Dungeness before throwing them into the pot. This conversation lead to other ideas we've come up with in the past – I know, you know, what I'm talking about. Everyone I know has had some kind of idea come to mind to improve something or to do something differently. Like a gas-powered turtleneck sweater or a fur sink for rich people (okay, not all ideas are smart ideas). Dennis was semi-retired and was a partner in a logistics company. He had experience in supply chain management and had worked with large electronics companies over the years. I decided to let him in on my world-changing invention/idea. I asked if he would be interested in hearing me out on a project I'd been working on for some years and would he be willing to sign an NDA (I would've told his wife without an NDA, but Dennis isn't Carol). I brought out my drawing and the formula pages, then we talked for hours.

We ended the weekend all excited. Dennis was going to start looking into product development companies that would build us a prototype.

I was going to do some searching for someone that could draw up what I was envisioning the device would look like.

Our research and schedule coordination took about 5 months. We sent a breakdown of the scope of work (SOW) we were interested in, in advance. We were scheduled to meet with two different prototype companies on a Monday in early December. Our first meeting was set-up for 10:00 a.m. in Seattle. These people were referred to Dennis by a University Business Advisor, who knew of a class of mechanical/design engineer students that would consider taking the project on as an experience project for the students, but overseen by experienced Engineers. We understood this would be a very cost effective way to get a prototype built.

The representatives of the first company arrived about 15 minutes early. We chatted and talked about how their program worked, while we waited for Dennis to arrive. By 10:15 and no Dennis, we decided to get started. Based on the SOW we provided them, they felt their team of students could handle the project. But the bad news was that it would take at least 6 months to complete as there were other projects they would be working on. The other good news was that they felt they could complete a working prototype for about $11,000. Wow, I thought, I wish Dennis was here to hear this. Then my phone rang, the display showed Dennis' name. I excused myself and took the call. It wasn't Dennis, it was his son-in-law, Sam. Sam explained that Dennis asked that he call me and apologize for his absence. I asked why Dennis didn't call, and Sam said he's at the emergency room, they believe he had a heart attack about 45 minutes earlier. "WHAT!!??" I quickly wrapped up the meeting, told the two gentlemen what had happened and that I needed to head to the hospital. I had all of their information and assured them we would follow-up with a conference call soon, and they understood.

I immediately postponed the other meeting Dennis and I had scheduled and waited for a call from Carol, Dennis' wife. Sam told me they were preparing to move Dennis to another hospital specializing in cardiac care. Once she called, I would head there. I had a pretty good idea what he and his family was going through, I too had a heart attack about four years earlier. I'm not sure if it's a requirement of inventors or just people trying to build a key loss prevention device. The first question out of Dennis' mouth when I saw him was, "So, how'd the meeting go?" I told him I wasn't inclined to share any of it with him if this is any indication of his reliability. I wanted to know if he was going to take this project seriously. He promised he'd straighten up and was determined to see this through. The good news is that Carol gave me *her* word on the matter. Dennis got to the hospital before any real damage occurred to his heart, a stent later and he was good to go (oh, yeah and a change in diet)!

Dennis took a little break through the new year and we jumped back into it in mid-January 2010. We met with a product design company called Slipstream Design. Jerry and Drew were a couple of extremely talented engineers. Dennis and I sat down with them for a couple of hours and talked about what I envisioned the device to look like, the features I wanted to see and the importance of its use being intuitive. I later learned that words like those are a tall order. After 3 or 4 more meetings to "tighten up" the features and design, Jerry and Drew gave us 12, 3-dimensional drawings of what the "Neely Device", could look like. This was the first time I could visually see a product (Fig. 3) coming to life.

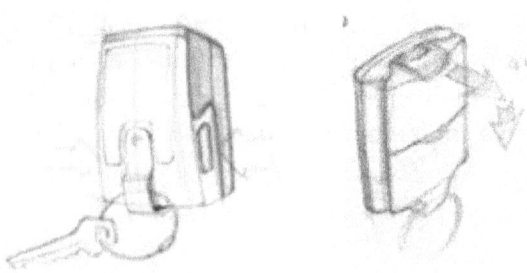

Fig. 3

The Key to Keys

Now that the form of the device was taking shape, it was important to find the company that was going to build the insides, mechanical and firmware engineers. Dennis and I interviewed two other companies at the recommendation of Jerry and Drew. They worked with these companies all the time and had their favorites, those they felt comfortable working with. Slipstream was designing the envelope or the casings (as they call it). It was imperative that the components and mechanical design the other company was going to propose would fit inside their casing.

Oh, and I had to name this thing. Neely Device wasn't going to cut it. I had the name in my head, but didn't know how to articulate it. I drew a picture of a stick person standing and a dotted line going from their waist to a ring of keys (really it was just a circle). Of course, the dotted line, in my head, represented a virtual string or cord. I then drew double curved arrows next to the keys showing that the keys could go around the user, but only so far. But I still didn't know what word would best describe the action. I couldn't sleep. Verbs were flying through my head. I had the drawing on my night stand, hoping I would come up with the word and I could immediately write it down ('cuz I would forget).

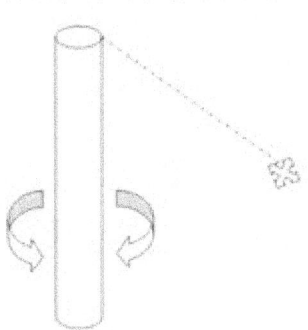

A device guaranteed to mitigate key loss.

Okay, I won't keep dragging this on, because it did take several days. I kept staring at the picture and I realized it looked like the old tetherball court in elementary school – THAT'S IT! **Tether** is the word I was searching for. This Neely Device was an Electronic Key Tether or **ekt**®! Once I figured it out, I used Microsoft Paint software to try and create a digital image (to the right).

How Much??!!

Remember the quote of $11,000 from the University students? The second company we sat down with, after reviewing in detail, the Scope of Work, came up with an estimate of between $175,000 - $300,000. This would get us 2 working prototypes and 10 finished or pilot devices. The third company, Product Creation Studios (PCS) came in considerably below the second bidder, but was still going to require a lot of money – after doing some reference checking, we were very impressed with PCS's reputation in the industry. Slipstream Design had done other projects with PCS and had worked with a few of their engineers in the past. We entered into agreements with both companies to take our idea to the prototype stage.

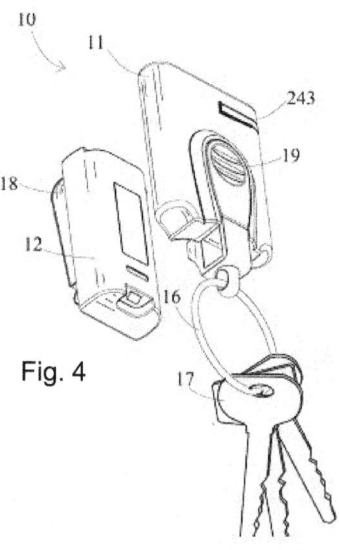

Fig. 4

I swear, I'm giving you the Readers' Digest version of this experience! Once Agreements were signed, Dennis and I were in on-going meetings about many details that I never would have thought about. Dennis attended many of the meeting with PCS on his own, while I was working with a start-up business attorney to create an LLC with the idea of raising funds to help cover any overruns and for production once we had a successful prototype. I then engaged with a different patent lawyer to conduct a search of like devices, as it had been 5 years since my last search. He would also work with the design, mechanical, electrical and firmware engineers in building the abstract for both a design and utility patent. I think it's important to note that during this same time, I was CEO of a regional contract security company with five branches in Washington and Oregon. It was a very busy time.

It took almost a year and several design iterations to reach our final product, the **ekt**® (Fig 4). Important features that we incorporated included:

Belt Unit
Strong carefully designed belt clip, similar to those used with gun holsters that are relatively easy to slide on your belt, but extremely difficult to remove.
Significant vibration when in alarm.
Off-tone chirping alarm when key unit is separated more than 5-7 steps.

Key Unit
85 dB alarm when separated from the belt unit by more than 5-7 steps.
Bright LED strobe light (1/2 watt) to ensure the User would immediately locate keys in both daylight and darkness.
Double-action motion in order to remove the key unit for preventing accidental separation.
Swivel key holder preventing key unit fob from getting in the way of using keys.

The **ekt**®'s casing is made out of a glass-filled nylon – rugged like the engine distributor caps of yesteryear. Each unit is powered by 2 'AAA' batteries with an estimated 4 to 6-month life. Once a battery reached a 20% capacity, it would begin to chirp alerting the User to change batteries, similar to a smoke detector action.

The distance of separation to alarm turned out to be the biggest challenge. The **ekt**® works like a two-way radio. Each unit communicates with the other. The trick was to measure the signal strength between the two units and when the signal dropped below a certain level, each unit would alarm. Sounds easy – NOT.

Our goal was for the device to alarm at about 5-7 steps (30-45 feet) of separation. This worked great when the belt and key units were set down in a room with a clear line of sight to each other. But problems began with real world testing. In actual use, the room's surroundings and particularly the human body would get in the way, reducing the signal strength and causing alarm. All one had to do was to wrap one's hand tightly around the key unit and oh-no, the device would alarm.

At this point, our options were to go back to square one or modify our design parameters. We elected to adjust the separation algorithm to accept a lower signal strength threshold to alarm. This solved the false alarming problem, but the distance to alarm now became 12-18 steps (40-55 feet) of separation. Although we weren't particularly thrilled with the trade-off, we deemed it necessary in order to eliminate the false alarms.

It was now late 2010. I had a good prototype, ready for production. We had identified an electronics company just outside of downtown Seattle that could manufacture the circuit boards and assemble the devices. They had the capacity to scale up on a short notice. There was also a mold company in eastern Washington that could crank out the casings. With the exception of having the initial mold forms made in Asia and a few of the electronics pieces, the **ekt**® would be made and assembled not only in the U.S., but in the State of Washington. That was important to me. Unfortunately, it also increased the COGS (*Cost of Goods Sold*), but in the end it was one of the smartest business decisions I made. The ability to drive to your assembly house and make changes instead of having to fly overseas to your manufacturing plant was huge. It also meant that we could build **ekt**® in small batches instead of the entire PO at once.

What's Next?

I was about out of money and still needed to get the **ekt**® licensed with the FCC and IC (Industry Canada), before it could ever be sold. If you look at most electronic gizmos, there will be a label on it that may show an FCC ID#, an IC# along or a CE mark (for Europe). In order to be allowed to use those stamps, the **ekt**® electronic specs would need to be reviewed and verified by the Agencies and a 'chamber test' conducted. The purpose of a chamber test is to ensure the radio frequency used and the device's other electronics do not interfere with Country standards, especially those used by emergency services and law enforcement. This is both an arduous and expensive task.

While Dennis continued to work with our vendors on final design, mold manufacturing, electronics building and warehousing, he also took on the job of designing a custom box for the **ekt**® to set in when shipped. I was working on developing a website with an e-commerce back-end, finalizing patent applications, filing for the **ekt**® trademark and preparing to raise money (i.e. bring on investors) in order to pay for producing the **ekt**®, and I needed to write a Business Plan and Executive Summary so potential Investors could envision a return on their investment. I had no idea what I was getting into, but I was learning quickly! All I wanted to do was prevent my guys from losing their keys.

Before I could consider asking people to invest in my little LLC, I needed to articulate what my invention was. I really didn't have a problem with that. Virtually everyone (99.5%) was able to grasp the concept and, like me, couldn't believe there wasn't a solution out there already. It's such a no-brainer. Transcribing that verbal discussion with people to a formal business plan was another thing. I was familiar with writing business plans throughout my years in the security industry, but those typically were in a format the Company used and contained elements they felt were important. I quickly found that writing a business plan for a start-up company, with investors in mind as the readers, was completely different. I searched for a business plan template geared towards start-up companies, having a product vs a service as the company's focus.

I sat down every night when I got home from work and wrote the Plan. There were some real head scratching topics that needed to be addressed, like a 5-Year financial pro forma, marketing plan, and management team. I really hadn't sat down and thought about those in detail. Again, I wanted something that would prevent people from losing their keys and I knew once I could build that, EVERYONE would want it; certainly everyone in my industry and that was a lot of units. But now I had to quantify some of those things. For example, how many sets of master keys are there in the United States? Where are they being used, e.g.: hospitals, casinos, jails, government, commercial real estate, schools? Wow, the more I thought about it, they're everywhere! Everyone is going to need this thing! I was getting real pumped imagining where this company and my invention could go.

After 6 nights of typing, I think I had covered just about everything anyone would want to know about the Problem, the Solution and how the **ekt**® was going to cure the industry's pain. They would understand my ideas for an initial marketing and product launch, what the financials would look like as the product was being produced, inventoried and sold. I had matrices, graphs, design images, a cool video and a beta website prospective investors could look at. I was introduced to a man named Bryan Brewer. He had a company called Business Plans Northwest. He specialized in helping entrepreneurs build Executive Summaries and Business Plans for start-ups. Especially those that were looking for investor funding. I felt it was critical I had someone intimately involved with writing start-up business plans look at mine before I started showing it around and I'm glad I did!

I met with Bryan at my office for a scheduled 1-hour meeting. Bryan asked me to "pitch" him like I would if I were asking for an investment. He knew nothing about my company or product. I had not yet shared my Business Plan with him. After explaining the Problem/Issue, Solution, etc., he "got it" right away. He asked to look at my plan and immediately said it would need to be reformatted. He recognized that it was a generic template I had found on the internet. He said it looked like it contained a lot of the information that would be needed, so a full re-write shouldn't be necessary. He also discussed the importance of having a 1 or 2-page Executive Summary that I could give people that would essentially pique their interest to learn more.

We also talked about the basic components of fundraising and how that process typically worked. First, entrepreneurs would go through a fundraising round called Friends and Family. It was not uncommon for a Start-up to go through other rounds, or tranches of fundraising, as their company built up. Brian mentioned that should I need to raise more money after my Friends and Family round, he could help navigate that path for me and help me build a Pitch Deck (a PowerPoint file) that synthesizes the key points of my business plan. He said one of the most common ways to raise money was through Angel Investor groups and there are many of them in the greater Puget Sound area.

Bryan took my Business Plan with him and got to work. While he cleaned up my Plan, I started building a list of the "Friends and Family" I would go to in order to pitch for an investment. Within about a month, I had my refreshed Business Plan, a one and two-page Executive Summary, a Pitch Deck and all the necessary legal documents needed to bring investors on. Just a note: Today a start-up company can use Crowdfunding websites, like Indiegogo, GoFundMe and Kickstarter to begin raising money. When I was going through this process, crowdfunding was not legal. Investors were required to meet IRS Rules (17 CFR 230.501) for an Accredited Investor. And just as I was getting ready to go, I learned about another term – Pre-Money Valuation.

What the heck is Pre-Money Valuation? A quick search on the Internet finds the following from Wikipedia: *A pre-money valuation is a term widely used in private equity or venture capital industries, referring to the valuation of a company or asset prior to an investment or financing. If an investment adds cash to a company, the company will have different valuations before and after the investment.*

In other words, to someone like me, Gobble de Goop. The good news is that the attorney I was using to create my business documents, Rex, helped me and we settled on a number, $1.2M. We came to this number by taking into consideration the amount of money my wife and I had personally invested so far, coupled with the fact that much of the product design and engineering were close to completion and soon to be in full production. That valuation was then converted to "units" (like Shares) of the Limited Liability Company.

Dennis knew what I was working on and all the details needed to begin fundraising. He and I would talk almost daily, briefing each other on what we learned that day and what more we needed to do to make this happen. During one of our update meetings, I told Dennis I was ready to contact Friends and Family and see if they were interested in putting in. We had a required minimum investment of $25,000. Before I was done telling him everything I had accomplished for this task, he said, "I'm not putting in – I just thought you should know." I said, "What? Are you kidding? After all of this?" Dennis replied, "I'm not, but Carol wants in – she believes in this, so we'll send you a check." That's Dennis – all loving, all caring, all the time! Forty-five days later, Dennis and I had raised just under $300,000 from Friends and Family – that was going to really get the ball rolling on production of our v1 (version 1), the **ekt**®.

I was advised to keep raising funds. Everyone experienced with start-ups and inventions said, "There are two important things to remember in this business: 1 – You'll need 2 or 3 times the amount of money you think you'll need and 2 – It's going to take 2 to 3 times longer to get things done." I really didn't believe that. I knew I had a built-in clientele, i.e.: my current clients and 2 years sounded like a more than reasonable amount of time to get the company built up and running.

Moving out of our Friends and Family round and on to the 'A' Round, I put together a list of Angel Investment groups and began applying to pitch before them in hopes of raising more money. I also entered into new product or entrepreneur contests to get some "free" advertising and recognition that I could use to impress potential new investors. Have you ever seen an episode of Shark Tank? With the exception of TV cameras and celebrity investors, pitching Angel Investors is done very much the same way. You apply with the Angel Group to pitch. Each Angel Group typically has a Gate Keeper – this person reviews your application, interviews you and gets an initial look at your presentation. If they're interested, they give you tips and suggestions on what you need to do to meet their requirements for pitching.

Sometimes you get blocked by the Gate Keeper. One of them I met with did not understand the need for the **ekt**®. He said that within a very short period of time all doors would be card access and there would be no need for hard keys. He just didn't see the point. I tried to explain that hard keys will always be around, as they are both super cheap and provide a failsafe in the event electronic access goes down. He still didn't buy it. He also didn't buy the argument that retrofitting the millions of buildings to electronic access in the near future wasn't possible. Long story short, I wasn't given the opportunity to pitch before his group of investors.

When you are given a date and time to pitch, there would usually be three or four other entrepreneurs pitching as well, unless you were at a "vetting" session where there could be 10 entrepreneurs pitching before a vetting board. That board would then pick four or five entrepreneurs to come back and pitch before the whole group at a later time. Depending on the group you were to pitch to, you were only allowed a specific amount of time. I've done as short as a 3-minute presentation to as long as 12 minutes (including Q&A). Basically, every Pitch Deck was required to address these topics:

The Problem
The Solution
Market Size
Go-to-Market Strategy
Financial Projections
Management Team
Investment Opportunity
Exit Strategy (how are investors going to get their money back)
Competition
Ask (this gave you the opportunity to tell the Group if there is something specific you are looking for that perhaps they could help with)

Over the next several months I had pitched to these Angel Groups:

Seraph Capital Forum, Puget Sound Venture Club, Zino Society, Northwest Entrepreneur Network, Technology Alliance and The Keiretsu Forum. I also won First Place at the Innovation Showcase – Seattle and won the NWEN's The First Look Forum event.

Things were moving at a fast pace, Anne, Dennis, and I were putting in very long hours every day. I would leave my office at 5:00 or 6:00 p.m., grab a fast bite and then meet Dennis and Anne at the next pitch or Entrepreneur wine mixer and then be home by 11:00pm.

The Key to Keys

The Keiretsu Forum, also known as K4, was the group I really wanted to pitch to. They are the largest Angel Investor group in the U.S. In the year I pitched to them, they claimed to be the catalyst for more than $24MM in private equity investments. K4 now has chapters around the world and their membership includes thousands of accredited investors. I found that different investment groups were interested in different types of investments. Some groups, for instance, were really focused on medical devices or breakthroughs, while others loved high tech gadgets or new snacks and foods entering the market. I remembered one particular pitch I did where I thought my presentation went very well until the next pitch was announced – the makers of POP popcorn. Everyone got huge samples and heard about Oprah loving the product. I was sunk. It can cost anywhere from $500 to $8,500 to make a pitch, so it was important to do as much research as you could on the group to be sure there was a fit for what you were going to pitch. Getting to know the Gate Keepers was very important.

It was mid-2012, before I got an opportunity to present before K4's vetting team. These investors would listen to a select few entrepreneurs' pitches and then vote, literally, while you were out of the room on who would be granted the opportunity to pitch before their entire group at a later date. I arrived about an hour early to be sure I could find parking and the conference room in this Class 'A' high-rise in downtown Seattle. I checked in at the pitch table and was led to another room where I was to wait with all the other Entrepreneurs. The room was full. I walked past the conference room where the pitches were being made. The room was enclosed in glass windows, but the windows had those frosted horizontal lines from end to end so you could tell something was going on but couldn't really see what. There was a lot of activity and you could hear applause now and again.

If I recall correctly, I had something like 8 minutes to make my pitch to be followed by 5 minutes of Q&A. There is a large digital clock facing you and the official Timer who would be sure you didn't go over. This

was standard practice at all of the pitches I had done. The only difference was the amount of time you got. They would tell you in advance so you had to practice to meet the time allotment before your actual pitch. Ten minutes before my turn, I was escorted to the outside hall "on deck" and waited for the vetting team to complete their discussion and score card for the last presenter.
I was ushered in and to the front of the room where the President of the NW Chapter of K4 introduced me. He reminded everyone (really just for my benefit) the rules of presenting and the time limit to keep in mind. When the clock ran out, I would be interrupted at whatever point I was at and the Q&A stage would begin. There had to be 18-20 people that made up this vetting group. It was hard to believe; this was just to get vetted. At other pitches I've done, there weren't usually more than 8 or 10 investors for the actual Pitch. This group was very professional – a large oval board room table that fit everyone around it, all with note pads, and with some of them already taking notes.

Every time I made a pitch to a group, as I was describing the **ekt®**, which I was wearing on my belt, I would remove the key unit from my belt, hold it up and show the audience what it looked like. I would then, by design, place the key unit on the podium or table next to me and finish my presentation. I couldn't have asked for a better conference room to present in. The conference room had an amazing view of downtown Seattle, all the buildings, everywhere, as well as the building that literally sat center of the view was one I had to rekey a few years earlier at a price of $80,000. As I described the "Problem" – I pointed outside to all the buildings and explained how many service employees are carrying master and sub-master keys as I spoke and how many of them will misplace them for a few minutes or hours, just today. Then I pointed to the big silver 900k SF high-rise right outside the window and how I was intimately familiar with what losing keys to that building meant.

I think I was able to articulate the problem well and I was able to demonstrate my expertise and familiarity in the contract service industry. The questions from the vetting team were good – I still got a few of the "But what about card keys?" I would explain that my security officers carry both hard keys and card keys and you can bet that both types of keys will be kept on an **ekt**® because I couldn't afford for a set of keys to go missing and it take hours before my officer knows they're even gone. Who might be using that card key while it's missing? What does it access – you still have a breach of security and someone is potentially using that card key to get into places s/he shouldn't be in. One of the Investors, sitting in the front definitely "got it" – he was telling the rest of the vetters that he had worked in the commercial property world for years and knew precisely what the pain was, not only for the vendor company that lost the keys, but for the property management company as well. They had to go to their tenants and the building owner when keys were lost and fess up to it. Tenants became very upset and the property management firm's reputation would take a hit. Even though the vendor company would ultimately have to pay for the rekey – the inconvenience to the tenants and the amount of time that inconvenience would last, was an extreme hassle. It felt good to hear someone explain the issues to the group as passionately as I did – I think that helped.

The last slide on my deck was titled "The Ask". This is where you have an opportunity to ask the panel of investors what you need to help bring your company to the next level. It could be advice on a particular topic or help reviewing some part of your Business Plan or financial metrics, etc. I told them I was looking for a seasoned CEO; one that had been through the experience of a start-up company along with an exit from that company. I began realizing as I went through these Shark Tanks that the process of bringing a product to Life PLUS managing an 800 employee company was too much. Anyone investing money in a start-up was going to want to be sure that there was someone working 100% on building the company and making it a success. I couldn't do it alone.

Anyway, my big finish came when I thanked everyone for their time and consideration. I ended by walking away from the podium, saying, "Can you imagine what it would be like if we never lost a set of master keys again?" And what happened as I got 12 steps away? My key unit, sitting on the podium would start alarming and the bright LED Strobe light flashing. I would say, "Oh shoot, my keys!" as I turned around to retrieve them. This got me a good laugh and a few "oohs".

I left the room feeling that my presentation before the K4 vetting committee went very well and my Big Finish went off without a hitch. But you don't learn right then and there whether you've passed the vetting group's scrutiny. Each of the committee members completes a scoring form. The form also notes their pros and cons about your pitch. The forms are collected and tabulated. A representative from the vetting group then contacts you to let you know the outcome of the vote.

The next day, I received a call from the K4 vetting group's Gate Keeper advising me that I was accepted to pitch before all of the Angels the next week. It was quite an honor, as later I learned that more than 30 companies had been vetted and only 6 were selected. I also received from individual group members some interest and questions in the days following the pitch. The best call I received, however, was from one of the Angels, John Suryan. John spent a number of years in the commercial property industry. In fact, the company he used to work for was a client of mine in Seattle for years. During my pitch to the vetting group, John was the one that explained to the other investors how real the pain is in the commercial high-rise market. That so many people, i.e.: janitors, security people, engineers, landlords, etc., are all carrying critical master and sub-master key sets. He validated my claim that misplacing a set of keys can be catastrophic. John told me that he enjoyed my presentation and could relate completely. He had founded a start-up called OfficeSpace.com, which he had exited from 18 months earlier and did well. He said he'd been looking at other opportunities and was deciding what he wanted to do next. He was intrigued by my "Ask" at the pitch for an experienced start-up CEO.

John and I met several times over the following two months and I'm happy to say that we came to an agreement and Tether Technologies (then known as **ekt**®, LLC) announced John Suryan as the new Chief Executive Officer! I felt an instant weight lifted off my shoulders. I didn't realize how much I was carrying, between serving as president of NW Protective and CEO of **ekt**®, let alone sitting on one non-profit Board, two HOA Boards, volunteering weekly with ElderFriends Northwest, *plus* preparing and serving breakfast for the homeless every month at Nativity House in Tacoma, WA. Frankly, my muscles are tensing just typing this. I bring this up only to note that we can easily add on tasks to our lives, not realizing the toll they may be taking on us. I learned the meaning of the term **burning the candle at both ends**. I really enjoy my extracurricular activities and bringing John on board allowed me to continue with those.

My "Ask" from the various Angel Groups had been for $1MM, to be used primarily to build and fund an inventory of 10,000 **ekt**® units. I was hoping that now with John on board, we could finally get the money. But one of the first things that John did was to change the Ask. He kept asking me, "Why build 10,000 units when we have no proof that the market will buy into your vision?" I bought into this logic and agreed that we should go with John's number of 2,000 units. This also meant that we could reduce the amount of money needed, down to as little as $250,000. For this lesser amount, we could retreat from the Shark Tank and go back to friends and family.

It was now September 1st and the new Ask started off with a bang. One of my investor friends agreed to invest $100k. John went to his network for the other $150k. Tooling for the **ekt**® casings was ordered. PO's for springs, latches, belt clips, printed circuit boards and final assembly were issued. All this activity and we had yet to come to year-end. By February (2013), we had 10 pre-production units in hand. We were so confident that $5,000 was spent on our **ekt**® launch party. We closed our second seed round in April with a total raise of $325k. With production finally underway, we looked to be in great shape.

It was now time for the rubber to hit the road. We exhibited at our first trade show, the NFMT (National Facilities Management & Technology), in Baltimore in March. Then it was ISC West (International Security Conference) in Las Vegas in April, followed by BOMA (Building Owners & Managers Association) in San Diego in June.

I purchased 40 **ekt**®s for use in some critical NW Protective accounts. Finally, I could sleep better at night, knowing the phone was less likely to ring with that dreaded call, "Randy, we can't find the keys, what do you want us to do?"

But the real thrill for me began when outside sales started to roll in. Others were buying into my vision and it wasn't just me with a pipe dream. By the time the ASIS trade show came about in the Fall, the company had sold over 200 **ekt**® devices to some big name customers: T-Mobile, University of Washington, Securitas Security and a VA Hospital in Bath, NY. I was smiling. But John was not. He had been chasing a 500-unit order from a very large company and had just been told that the **ekt**® did not meet their needs.

In the preceding 12 months, we were successful in obtaining a design patent on the **ekt**®, trademarking the name "EKT®" and we had raised hundreds of thousands of dollars. We changed the name of the Company from **ekt**®, llc to Tether Technologies, Inc. The domain name, tethertech.com, was acquired for $1,000. Sales of the **ekt**® were solid but nowhere near what we had wanted them to be. There many, many Pros we got from customers, but there were two common Cons. Customers said that if they could change anything about the device, then these were the two things. One was its size; they wanted it smaller so that it was not so "bulky" when worn and so that it would fit into a key cabinet. Two was the distance-to-alarm; they wanted it shortened.

So in the fall of 2013, we decided to pivot and go to work on a smaller unit which we dubbed "v2". John tapped his network and recruited two individuals to join the company. We were going to need to raise more money to which Sam Traff became our Chief Operating Officer. To address customer feedback for a smaller unit, we brought on Keith Kirkwood as our VP of Product Development.

Sam has been involved in many successful Start-ups and has significant resources when it comes to raising money. In addition to working on projects together over the years, Sam and John had gone to the University of Washington together, both becoming CPAs and diving deep into the entrepreneur-world early on. Keith brought more than 30 years of experience in product development and electronics packaging with him. As we explained the **ekt**® to him, along with our design goals for v2, he became confident that we could reduce the size of the unit and shorten the tether distance to alarm.

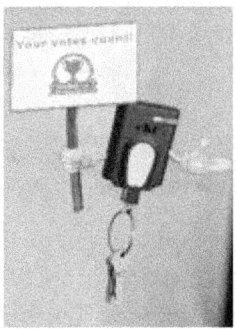

Sam rewrote the business plan and re-did the financial projections. John pulled together the funding documents we were going to need. Keith came up with a "form-factor" design, which was basically the envelope v2 would aspire to. The four of us, later dubbed, the Four Amigos by our spouses and investors, continued entering contests and exhibiting at different industry tradeshows around the country. We interviewed with the Puget Sound Business Journal technology reporter, now Editor-in-Chief, to enter the Journal's first ever, TechFlash Cup competition in 2013. This was a competition of 16 Start-ups and 5 inventors. The contest lasted 6 weeks with two companies being eliminated every week. Articles about each company were published in the Technology Section of the weekly Journal. Readers were asked to log on to a special competition URL and vote, every day, on which companies were their favorite.

To prompt our followers to vote every day (for 6 weeks) we turned our **ekt**® into **Mr. ekt**® who would remind them each day by email! Once they voted they would get the "I voted today for **ekt**®" badge/button that they could proudly, uh, look at!

All of the articles and voting built up to a final award of the TechFlash Cup one evening at Seattle's Triple Door theater. There were only four (4) companies left (and we were one). The winner was selected based on each companies' efforts, comments from the public over the six-week period and input from a panel of five judges, influential individuals from the start-up community, including Angel Investors and Venture Capitalists.

While we did not win the TechFlash Cup – we did receive significant accolades – garnering more than 20,000 on-line votes and being awarded "The People's Choice" of the competition. It was an honor to make the final four.

By December 2013, we were ready to go back into the "Shark Tank". John is an experienced Angel Investor and understands that world. He was able to move easily through the Angel Investor labyrinth. Our efforts began paying off. At the same time, we changed the company name to Tether Technologies, we made a strategic decision to convert from an LLC (Limited Liability Company) to an S-Corp and finally to a C-Corp, which then allowed us to accept money from entities and not just individuals. Not only did this open up a larger pool of investors, but entities tend to make bigger investments.

It was a real achievement obtaining the IP (Intellectual Property) around my invention and keeping the production, assembly and distribution, here in the United States. Patent laws are not universally respected in all countries. The more you can keep "at home" the better. But it was paramount that we listened to customer feedback, to the end-users in the field (like my security officers), and acted accordingly. Keith began building a plan for v2 (later called the *Gravity*). John, Sam, Keith and I met to review preliminary drawings and proposed technology changes Keith was working on. The great news is that we would be able to use our IP or "secret sauce" for this version as well. The signaling technology would change from RF (Radio Frequency) to BLE (low energy Bluetooth). This moved us to an international standard vs. having to change RF for different countries/markets. With BLE, we could also build a communications link with smart phones.

Another important new feature was to add an accelerometer to the key unit. This allowed us to use motion in the separation algorithm. When the keys are moving (in the hand of the user), the signal strength threshold to alarm is reduced. This allowed us to both shorten the tether distance and have better consistency in the distance to alarm. We were on our way to achieving the 5-7 steps of tether distance that I had set forth in the initial design specs for the **ekt**®.

Further, Keith felt that we had an opportunity to reduce the size of the overall unit by 40%! There were two main factors that would allow that: First, going to a chip antenna from a PCB antenna reduced the internal real estate required, and second, better understanding of the power requirements of the alarms and rumble/vibrator would allow us to eliminate one "AAA" battery from *both*, the Key and Belt units (the original **ekt**® was overpowered). We would see further size reduction by changing the design of the device from a "stacked" fit to a "nested" fit. Below is a visual comparison of the v1 vs. v2 concept.

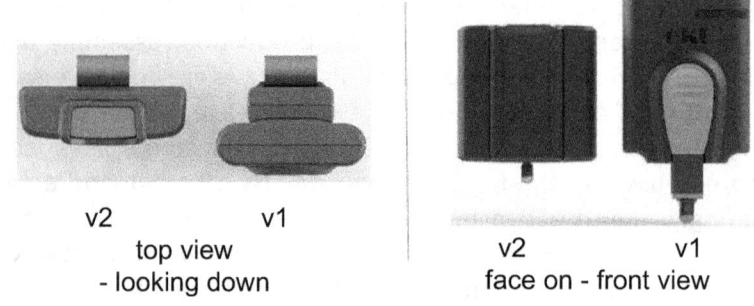

v2   v1
top view
- looking down

v2   v1
face on - front view

Keith began building 3D prototypes for us to test. We shared these prototypes and renderings with existing **ekt**® customers to get their opinions and suggestions. This design was well received and with some minor tweaks, the product development process began in earnest. Along the way, we went through patent protection, material selection, firmware coding and FCC/IC licensing. As these things were completed, we met with many of our **ekt**® customers and offered discounts to early-adopters of the new version – in fact, we ultimately decided to offer the *Gravity* at a ~15% - 20% reduced retail price over the **ekt**® to grab market share.

The Key to Keys

One of my objectives with both **ekt**® and *Gravity* was to manufacture them in the USA. With **ekt**®, we hired two local companies. The first, Cascade Quality Molding ("CQM"), located in Yakima, WA. CQM was responsible for the plastic casings, metal parts, springs and belt clips. For the printed circuit boards ("pcbs") and final assembly, we used a Seattle-based company, Schippers & Crew. CQM's true expertise was in plastics. They had a shop in China where the molds for the plastics were made. We considered making the molds in the U.S., but that would have cost us 3x, or an additional $100,000. The molds were loaded on a ship and after an 8-week journey, they arrived in Yakima, WA. The **ekt**® plastics were made from glass filled nylon, which turned out great.

The metal parts and belt clips were another story. CQM sourced those parts from other Chinese factories, which later we found, they had little control over. We had two major service bulletins with **ekt**®. The first was regarding the belt clip. In order to hold it in place, the clip had a small prong that bent out from the back at approximately a 10-degree angle. The clip would slide in between two rail slots on the back of the belt unit. Once installed, the prong would lodge into a divot in the plastic, thus securing the clip in place.

Shortly after we began shipping finished **ekt**®s to customers, we started to hear reports of the entire **ekt**® unit falling off the belt of the user. In fact, we had one customer send us a photo of their **ekt**® lying on the ground next to a storm drain, almost having lost their key set. As we assessed the situation, we determined that there were significant inconsistencies in the prong angle. As we inspected un-assembled clips, we found many with prong angles below 5 degrees. What followed was our first service bulletin, "Belt Clip Inspection." Customers were asked to pry up on their belt clips and if the clip dislodged, to bend out the prong and re-insert the clip. We then added a step to our manufacturing process to bend out all prongs prior to installing the clip.

The second service bulletin falls into the category of "You've got to be kidding me." During the testing of our first **ekt**® prototype, we found that the **ekt**® would prevent some keys from turning the lock completely around. To fix this, a swivel was added to the bottom of the pawl. Everything looked good. But again, after six months of **ekt**® being in the field, we started to get reports of keys falling off. You would think that was a death sentence to a device designed to prevent you from losing your keys. But our customers hung with us. We inspected the situation and determined that the cap on top of the swivel would wear out, causing the swivel to fall from the pawl. We sent out an alert to our customers, remade the swivel using a U.S. company, and produced a replacement part within two months.

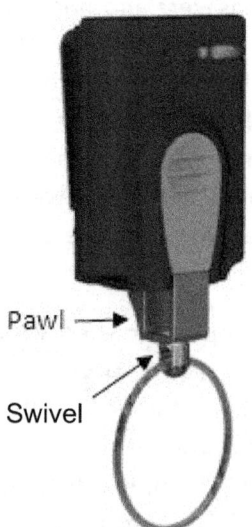

The trials and tribulations of the **ekt**® has had a major impact on our manufacturing and testing of *Gravity*. A book called "*Poorly Made in China*" by Paul Midler was recommended to me. Had I read that before dealing with an unknown company in China, I believe I would've avoided major delay, inconveniences to our customers and saved thousands of dollars. If you have a product that you think would be great to source overseas, be sure to read this book. I strongly suggest that before you engage in manufacturing of any kind, in China or outside of the U.S. for that matter, be sure you know the company you're dealing with and be sure they are not relying on other companies that you don't know to produce your final product.

As a result of this experience, all of **Gravity**'s metal parts, except for the belt clip, are made by US companies. **Gravity** plastics are molded in China by a company that had done work for Keith in the past. Keith recommended that we shoot our first set of plastics in China in case any changes need to be made to the molds (based on our first manufacturing run). It's ironic to me that U.S. laws are written in such a way that if the outside of your product is not made in the U.S. (and even though everything else is), then it must be labeled as *Assembled in USA*. Even though the **ekt®** had more dollar-value components made overseas, we were still able to label it as *Made in USA* due to the fact that the casings were molded in Yakima, WA.

Another big learn from **ekt®** was the amount of beta and pilot testing that **Gravity** went through. The **ekt®** went from first manufacture directly to customers in less than a month. **Gravity** went from first manufacture to beta testing to pilot build to production build to customers over the course of six months. It was subjected to a series of tests, including drop, vibration, temperature, humidity and ESD (electrostatic discharge). During pilot unit testing (by customers out in the field), we had two key unit failures due to water, rendering the pcb inoperable. In our production process, we now add a conformal coating to the pcb. As a result, there have been zero moisture related **Gravity** failures to date. During this six-month testing period, several other minor tweaks were made to the product design and the firmware. The result is a less than 2% failure rate of the Gravity.

Further, we now have very close relationships with overseas manufacturers, some of whom are investors in Tether Technologies and clearly have a vested interest in our success. It makes a difference when you KNOW who you're working with.

In October of 2015, we launched the new *Gravity* Key Tether at the American Society for Industrial Security (ASIS) Annual Conference and Tradeshow. As mentioned in earlier chapters, there are a lot of clients that have invested in electronic key control cabinets. A technology that tracks to whom keys have been issued, offers management metrics and notifications when a set of keys have not been returned by the time expected and controls who can access what set of keys. One of the problems with the v1, **ekt**®, is that the unit was so large, it would not easily fit into these expensive key control cabinets. These clients realize that with the cabinets, they know who has the keys and when they're due back, but what they don't have is a means of preventing users from misplacing or losing the keys. Without incorporating the **ekt**®, their key control program has a big hole; likewise, without the **ekt**® being able to fit in key control cabinets, we were missing out on an opportunity to help customers close the loop on the missing piece of key control. Well, we fixed that with the *Gravity*!

With both the **ekt**® and the *Gravity*, there are two parts to the device(s), the Belt Unit and the Key unit. Each unit is uniquely paired to each other. You can be in a room with hundreds of *Gravity* devices and none of them will interfere or miscommunicate with the other. They each communicate only with their paired "partner". With the *Gravity*, we developed an optional Un-Pairing station. This allows the client to un-pair the Key Unit from the Belt Unit, essentially, putting the key unit to sleep and turning off the belt unit. Once un-paired, the user can toss the belt unit in a drawer and hang the key unit (with the keys attached) in the key box. There is no risk of an alarm when separating the two units.

The Key to Keys

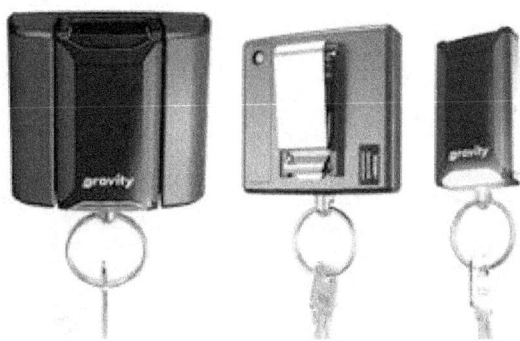

We recognized, however, that if someone were to remove a sleeping key unit from the electronic key cabinet, they could theoretically walk away with them and they would not be paired with a belt unit, risking misplacement or loss. Fortunately, the accelerometer we had previously added to the key unit's separation algorithm could be used again. So now, after the belt and key units are unpaired and the key unit is hanging in the box, if the key unit is moved, or senses motion for 10 seconds of continual motion, it will alarm until paired with a belt unit or left alone and still.

We believe that these improvements, the smaller size and decrease in the tether distance have answered the requests that end-users asked for in a new version. We believe **Gravity** is a real game-changer – it fits the bill of all those end users out there looking to take their key control program to the next level. We believe that over time, the **Gravity** will become to physical security and key control, what smoke detectors are to fire and life safety – A Must Have.

EPILOGUE

An epitaph on the **ekt**®. Whenever you bring a new product to market, you never know how long it will last or if there will be warranty issues or a fatal flaw that brings death. For **ekt**®, it was the massive improvement in the v2 *Gravity* that caused its demise. **ekt**® turned out to be a very durable product. I know of several customers that continue to use it today, and in fact, prefer its larger size (akin to a big stick on the restroom key). Had we built 10,000 units as I had initially set forth to do, I would not be here writing this book. Tether Technologies would have run out of money and died, as 95% of new businesses do. Instead, we ended up building 461 devices, selling 373 units, giving away 68 as demos or warranty replacements, and if my math is right, having about 20 left in (obsolete) inventory. We only had to take a $10k write off on obsolete component parts as we closed out our 2,000 unit **ekt**® PO 1,539 units short of completion.

The epitaph on *Gravity* has yet to be written. So far, we are off to a great start. *Gravity* sales surpassed in six months what it took two years with **ekt**® to accomplish. Warranty returns/repairs are less than 2%. The early feedback has been very positive:

> "Simple to use, low maintenance, & can alleviate a lot of potential headaches down the road." Regional Technology Director, National Contract Security Provider

> "This product has lived up to its reputation. We feel this is an important tool that can really benefit our teams as we carry keys on a round the clock basis." Regional Manager, premier east coast Security company

60-unit purchase after comparison of the **Gravity** to "item finder" apps, major State University campus with more than 30,000 undergraduate enrollments.

"*I am using two of the **Gravity** units and they work great. The technical support is fantastic. I greatly recommend this product.*" Account Manager, multi-state security and investigations firm

"*I am excited to get these in use so we can prevent the next lost master key.*" Branch Manager, Global Security Provider

21 unit purchase used in conjunction with key control cabinet, ensuring keys are returned at the end of each shift. 750,000 sq. ft., Class 'A' high-rise, Pacific Northwest

"*I wear mine every day and require others to do the same. This device is a game-changer in my opinion. In our field testing, the learning curve is absolutely flat and requires little to no training.*" Lead Facility Engineer, NW HVAC Mechanical contractor.

"*It's a very small investment to protect our reputation. Our clients love it, our field personnel love it, our managers love it, and we plan to purchase more.*" National Director, Healthcare Security

"*I'm able to create a competitive edge over other security companies who haven't found out about the **Gravity** yet. And in our highly competitive industry, I want to create every advantage I can.*" Regional Vice President, national protection agency

"*The **Gravity** solution provides premier companies, like ours, the best overall protection against high costs associated with a set of lost master keys. We'd rather focus our resources on key loss prevention technology than on paying high insurance deductibles.*" Branch Manager, one of the Top Three Global Security Providers

I can absolutely say that if **Gravity** had been in use in the first two True Stories above, neither of them would have happened. In Story I, as soon as the security rover walked away from the vending machine, **Gravity** would have alarmed. The rover would have turned around and retrieved the keys, probably without even breathing a sigh of relief. In Story II, as soon as the keys ended up in the dumpster, the janitorial supervisor would have been alerted. In Story III, since it was never determined how the keys were lost, I can't say for sure. But I'm willing to bet 100 **Gravitys** that key loss would also have been averted. As far as the Other Headlines Worth Pondering, you be the judge. But I'm willing to bet 100 more **Gravitys** on each one of those too. Want to take me up on that wager?

In conclusion, I am super excited to bring **Gravity** to my network of security professionals. My career started at a high-end resort in San Diego. While still in college, I was hired as a security officer. A few years later, my family decided to move to the Bay Area. I worked the first year or so as a Private Investigator – not my cup of tea. I reached out to my former Chief of Security at the resort in San Diego, and he contacted a friend of his who oversaw corporate security operations for ABM Security in San Francisco. After a couple of interviews, I was hired as a Field Inspector. My job was to go from account to account and make unscheduled, unannounced, inspections of the security officers assigned to the accounts. It was also my job to respond to job sites where officers were reporting that they couldn't find their keys!

I spent close to five years with ABM in the Bay Area – from Field Inspector, District Manager and Operations Manager to Branch Manager of their Santa Clara branch. I was then given the opportunity to become a regional manager with an office located in the Seattle. It was an opportunity I couldn't refuse. My role with ABM Security grew larger and included opening and managing branches in 5 States and overseeing all contract security operations nationally for one of the world's largest high tech companies headquartered in the Puget Sound area. In 2007, I was recruited away by NW Protective Service to serve as their President and CEO. My mission was to bring this 67-year-old, family-owned company, on to a level playing field in terms of technology, service delivery and offerings, that the big national companies were offering their clients. But more importantly, increase the value of the company, placing it in a position to be acquired. In April 2015, NW Protective was purchased by Universal Protection Service.

I stayed on with Universal through the earn-out period to ensure my clients continued to receive exemplary service and attention as the two companies transitioned. I'm please to say NW Protective was paid more than the agreed upon sales price for the company, as not only did we retain 100% of the clients during the transition, but we were successful in bringing on other accounts, some quite large, during the transition. The acquisition was a win-win for both NW Protective and Universal. I made some good friends with Universal during the transition. Real professionals that understood the business like I did. I tendered my resignation, the first time in September of 2015. I was excited to begin working full-time for Tether Technologies as the launch of our v2 **Gravity** key tether was really starting to take off. Universal pressed hard for me to stay on and I did for another 5 months to help as they acquired four more security companies. I ended up resigning in January 2016 in order to pursue my true passion, the elimination of master key loss by security officers.

I can't wait to get up in the morning. I love calling my former security colleagues to tell them what I'm up to. The typical reaction is, "WOW, that's awesome, do you know how long I've been looking for something like that?" My goal is to make **Gravity the new standard of care** in key control management. Imagine you are a security director having to explain a lost set of keys when confronted with the fact that there is a system out there that prevents exactly that from happening.

The Key to Keys

If you're reading this, congratulations and thank you for making it all the way though my book. Now the next thing you need to do is take action – eliminate the risk of key loss – buy **Gravity** at www.stopkeyloss.com. Use the discount code **key2keys16** to save 10% on your first **Gravity** purchase.

About the Author

Randy Neely is founder of Tether Technologies, Inc. Having spent more than 40 years in the security and property management industries, Randy saw a glaring need for a key control program that would actually _prevent_ the loss of keys. On multiple occasions, Randy dealt with situations where master keys were lost or misplaced, ultimately costing facility owners tens of thousands of dollars in re-keying expenses. The ability to eliminate those situations drove Randy to develop the idea for Tether Technologies' **ekt**® (an electronic key tether), the **Gravity** Key Tether and the ID Tether.

Since 2007, Randy was the CEO of Northwest Protective Service, a regional security company in the Northwest. Previously, he was vice president of a national security company for 21 years. Randy also managed residential and high-rise properties in Southern California and worked in the proprietary section of the security field in the hospitality industry. Randy is the past president of the Washington State Security Council.

www.ingramcontent.com/pod-product-compliance
Lightning Source LLC
Chambersburg PA
CBHW060348190526
45169CB00002B/526